BROKE TO

BILLIONAIRE

HOW TO MAKE MONEY ONLINE WITH AI

BRANDON CHAN

Disclaimer Notice

Please note the information contained within this document is for educational and entertainment purposes only. Every attempt has been made to provide accurate, up-to-date, reliable, and complete information. No warranties of any kind are expressed or implied. Readers acknowledge that the author is not engaging in the rendering of legal, financial, medical, or professional advice. The content of this book has been derived from various sources. Please consult a licensed professional before attempting any techniques outlined in this book.

While the title and content of this book are crafted to inspire and guide readers towards financial success in the online realm using AI, it is essential to understand that the term "billionaire" is metaphorical. By no means is this book promising or guaranteeing that readers will attain billionaire status, or any specific financial milestone, for that matter. The strategies and insights provided are tools to foster growth and prosperity in the digital age, and outcomes will vary based on individual effort, market dynamics, and other external factors.

Ethical Considerations for Using AI:

Artificial intelligence offers a plethora of opportunities, but with great power comes great responsibility. As users and proponents of AI, we must be aware of the ethical implications and responsibilities tied to its utilization. This includes ensuring that AI applications respect user privacy, promote fairness, and avoid perpetuating biases. Additionally, while AI can augment human capabilities, it is crucial to use it as a complementary tool rather than a replacement for human judgment and values. As we harness the potential of AI, we urge readers to approach its application with discernment, integrity, and a genuine commitment to the betterment of society.

By reading this document, the reader agrees that under no circumstances is the author responsible for any losses, direct or indirect, which are incurred as a result of the use of the information contained within this document, including, but not limited to, errors, omissions, or inaccuracies.

TABLE OF CONTENTS

INTRODUCTION

Picture this: It is a new day, and not just any day; it is a day where the mysteries of technology and the aspirations of humans come together in beautiful harmony. You're not just a bystander in this dance; you're center-stage, equipped with the potent tools of artificial intelligence. And this isn't some futuristic fantasy; it's the present. Here, you can smoothly merge multiple income streams and create an intricate, yet robust, web of online wealth.

Sure, you've heard of ChatGPT, but this journey is only the beginning. From the rhythmic algorithms of TikTok to the deep waters of SEO, the vast expanse of YouTube, the bustling marketplace of Amazon KDP, and the fast-paced lanes of Instagram, the possibilities are endless. *Broke to Billionaire: How to Make Money Online with AI* is crafted meticulously by Brandon Chan, an AI aficionado and your digital entrepreneur guide. His love for AI is as vast as the digital universe itself, and he is here to share it with you in all its wonder and complexity.

Don't mistake this for another run-of-the-mill guide. It's a comprehensive exploration that goes beyond mere steps and strategies. It is a blend of wisdom and practicality—a combination of engaging, easy-to-follow steps with real-life examples, all woven together with an expert's touch. And for those new to the AI space, fear not, because the *Broke to Billionaire* (Free Prompt Guide) is like a comforting hand on your shoulder, steering you through the maze of ChatGPT and beyond.

But hold on to your space helmets-because this journey isn't just about leveraging AI. It's also about understanding its soul. Brandon takes you deep into the ethical galaxies, exploring critical issues surrounding AI usage and ensuring that your path to financial independence is prosperous and conscientious. Learn about the legal constellations and responsible AI deployment to make your mark on the future morally and ethically.

However, let's ground ourselves for a moment. While the sky's the limit, Brandon's guidance remains grounded. Rather than selling you dreams of passive earnings, he offers reality, an authentic blueprint to financial and time freedom. It's not a magic potion but a carefully designed map with opportunities aiming for true economic freedom. This isn't about fleeting success; it's about sustainable prosperity.

To the aspiring entrepreneurs wondering if they have a place in this new world, to the freelancers hoping to expand their horizons, and to anyone longing for side hustles that don't just promise but deliver, this book is your beacon. Within its pages lies not just a wealth of information but also the heart and soul of AI. It's not just about making money online; it's about embracing the future, understanding its power, and making it your own. With Brandon's words as your guide, the world of AI isn't just a possibility; it's a promise waiting to be fulfilled.

What is AI ?

1. A Quick Dip into the World of AI:

At its core, AI is a computer system trained to perform tasks that typically require human intelligence. Think of it as a diligent student, absorbing and learning from limitless amounts of data, but without the coffee breaks or distractions.

2. A Blast From the Past:

If you thought AI was the cool new kid on the block, think again! AI's roots can be traced back to the mid-20th century. Alan Turing, often deemed the father of modern computing, once asked, "Can machines think?" With that simple question, the wheels of AI innovation began to turn.

3. Fast Forward to Today: Beyond ChatGPT:

From Siri to Netflix recommendations, AI is everywhere. I remember when ChatGPT was the talk of the town—a marvel in conversational AI. Now, it's just one of the myriad tools showing how far we've come. And while ChatGPT can spin a good yarn, other AIs are driving cars, diagnosing diseases, or even predicting the weather!

4. Gazing into the Crystal Ball: AI's Future:

The future of AI is limitless! Aspiring entrepreneurs might find themselves brainstorming ideas with an AI partner. Or, perhaps, AI will compose symphonies that tug at our heartstrings. The key takeaway? The possibilities are endless, and the journey, well, it's just getting started.

5. The Magic of Possibilities:

I believe that the power of AI lies in its potential to redefine possibilities. Need a personal stylist? There's an AI for that. How about a virtual assistant to manage your multiple streams of income? Check! AI is not just about automation; it's about augmentation. It's not about replacing us; it's about empowering us.

CONCLUDING THOUGHTS

With great power comes great responsibility. The world of AI is mesmerizing but comes with its own set of challenges. Legal and ethical considerations, responsible AI deployment, and understanding the critical issues surrounding AI usage are all crucial

CHAPTER 1

SELLING PRINT-ON-DEMAND
WITH ETSY

"Success is not the key to happiness. Happiness is the key to success. If you love what you are doing, you will be successful." - Albert Schweitzer

Ai, Etsy, and Print-on-Demand:

I magine a marketplace that celebrates creativity, champions the spirit of handmade goods, and connects artisans to customers worldwide. If you're thinking of Etsy, then you're spot on! Let's unravel the magic that is Etsy.

Founded in 2005, Etsy started with a simple idea: create a community driven platform where crafters could sell their handmade goods to a global audience. But, like any thriving ecosystem, it didn't take long for Etsy to evolve. Over the years, this Brooklyn-based startup has transformed into a bustling global marketplace, featuring everything from handcrafted jewelry to custom-designed clothing and even antique treasures that span decades. With over 60 million items listed, Etsy became a global go-to for unique finds.

But wait, there's more to Etsy than just its rich history. The platform's adaptability is genuinely commendable. And it's not just a hub for vintage and handmade items anymore. Thanks to technological advancements, Etsy has opened doors for entrepreneurs looking to sell "print-on-demand" products. Ah, the beauty of the digital age! It's this adaptability, combined with its dedication to supporting small businesses, that makes Etsy a shining star in the world of e-commerce.

For those of you still wrapping your heads around "print-on-demand", let's break it down. This business model designs a product and has it produced only after a customer places an order. It's like running a bakery where cookies are baked only when someone's at the counter, cash in hand, craving that chocolate chip goodness. Think of it like this: instead of investing heaps of cash into bulk printing and then crossing your fingers hoping the items sell, you wait. Wait for an order, then have that singular product printed and shipped. It's efficient, it's economical, and it's environmentally conscious. And the best part? With the power of AI (which we'll delve deeper into later), creating these designs becomes an innovative adventure.

Setting up an Etsy store is like opening a digital storefront, where your shop's aesthetics merge seamlessly with its functionality. Behind its artsy facade, the platform offers an array of tools designed to help sellers manage their inventory, track sales, communicate with customers, and gain insights to boost their business. It blends artistic endeavors with the tech world's efficiency.

But you might wonder, with millions of sellers already on Etsy, is there room for one more? To which I'd say, in the ever-expanding universe of e-commerce, there's always room for passionate entrepreneurs with a unique voice and a splash of creativity. And with the assistance of AI, standing out from the crowd has become a tad bit easier. Think of Etsy as an ever-expanding digital city, and in this city, there's a neighborhood perfect for your brand.

So buckle up as we explore the marvel of Etsy, infused with a sprinkle of AI magic. From its rich history to its adaptability to changing times, Etsy promises a haven for budding entrepreneurs. Let's turn your creative ideas into a profitable venture, shall we?

Benefits of Integrating AI into Print-on-Demand

So, you've wrapped your head around Etsy and the sheer genius of the print-on-demand model. Now, let's stir some AI magic into this concoction and see how it turns the entire game on its head.

1. **Elevated Design Capabilities:** Ever had a day when the creative juices just weren't flowing? We all have those moments! But here's where AI comes to the rescue: With AI-driven design tools, you get a plethora of design suggestions based on current trends, themes, or even a mood you're aiming for. Think of AI as that artsy friend who never runs out of inspiration and always has a fresh perspective. And the best part? This artsy friend is available around the clock. No more waiting for that eureka moment; AI provides a continuous flow of ideas.

2. **Tailored Product Recommendations:** Picture this: a customer stumbles upon your shop because of a quirky t-shirt design they love. Now, wouldn't it be fabulous if you could suggest similar or complementary products they

might be interested in? AI algorithms can analyze buying patterns and preferences to serve up spot-on recommendations, increasing their chances of buying more. The sophistication here is incredible; it's not just about what others bought but a deep understanding of individual preferences. It's like having a savvy sales assistant who knows every customer's taste!

3. **Optimized Pricing:** Determining the right price can be a conundrum. Price it too high, and you might deter customers; price it too low, and you risk underselling your creativity. AI analyzes market trends, competitor pricing, and demand to suggest the sweet spot that maximizes profits while remaining appealing to customers. Beyond just the numbers, AI provides context and insights into the why and how of pricing dynamics. It's like having a seasoned market expert whispering pricing secrets in your ear.

4. **Efficient Inventory Management:** While print-on-demand reduces the need for vast inventories, there's still the challenge of managing different designs, sizes, and product types. AI can forecast which designs will likely be hot sellers and help you manage resources effectively. Gone are the days of gut feelings. With AI, every decision is data-backed. Like a crystal ball giving a tiny glimpse into future sales trends, that's AI for you.

5. **Enhanced Customer Engagement:** In the digital world, engagement is gold. AI chatbots can answer customer

queries instantly, offer personalized shopping advice, and even gather feedback. These aren't your standard pre-programmed responses; AI bots can understand context, emotion, and even humor. It's like having a 24/7 customer service rep who never takes a coffee break and always has a smile on their face (or, well, their interface).

6. **Strategic Marketing Insights:** Want to know the best time to launch a new design? Or which of your products is getting the most attention? AI analytics go beyond mere numbers. They can provide deep insights into customer behavior, uncovering patterns you'd never have spotted on your own. This knowledge empowers you to make informed marketing decisions. It's akin to having a backstage pass to your customer's mind.

7. **Let the magic of innovation and AI propel your Etsy store to stardom!** To cap it off, integrating AI into your print-on-demand venture isn't just about adding a few fancy tools. It's about supercharging your business, redefining boundaries, and pushing the horizons of what's possible. As we navigate the vast sea of online entrepreneurship, remember that AI is your copilot, ensuring you soar to new heights with every opportunity.

So, let's tap into the marvel of this technology and redefine the boundaries of what's achievable.

Tools Spotlight: AI-Driven Marvels for Printon-Demand

After scouring the depths of the internet, I bring you some dazzling AI tools for your print-on-demand journey. Presenting your digital sidekicks, ready to amplify your creative prowess:

1. DeepArt.io:

What it's for: Transforming photos into artwork.

How it works: Whether it's Van Gogh's starry swirls or Warhol's pop art you're after, DeepArt brings a touch of classic artistry to your designs.

2. Lumen5:

What it's for: Video content creation for products.

How it works: Convert those text descriptions into vibrant video narratives. Lumen5 crafts visual stories tailored to your product, making your designs not just seen but experienced.

3. Crello:

What it's for: Design and animation.

How it works: As your on-call graphic designer, you can feed Crello a theme and get back a flurry of design elements and animations. Perfect for those captivating store banners and promotional materials.

4. Everbee:

What it's for: Automated design creation.

How it works: Everbee's AI processes trends and popular designs to suggest fresh, market-ready creations. It's like having a personal design assistant who's always in the know.

5. RelayThat:

What it's for: Brand consistency in designs.

How it works: Maintain a consistent look and feel across all your products. Input your brand elements— colors, fonts, logos—and RelayThat ensures every design harmonizes with your brand voice.

6. Printful's Mockup Generator:

What it's for: Product mockup visualization.

How it works: A gem for visualizing your designs in the real world. See how they'd look on T-shirts, mugs, posters, and more— basically, a digital fitting room for your art.

7. Visme's Infographic Maker:

What it's for: Infographic designs.

How it works: It broadens your design horizon with engaging infographics. Feed in your data or theme, and Visme crafts the visual story for you.

8. Midjourney:

What it's for: Scouting and predicting design trends.

How it works: Midjourney's AI keeps a pulse on the market, sniffing out emerging design trends and making sure you're always a step ahead of the curve.

9. Canva:

What it's for: User-friendly design platform.

How it works: Canva's pro version comes packed with a magic resize feature, a brand kit, and a content planner, all enhanced with AI to streamline your design process. Whether you are a newbie or a seasoned designer, Canva is a must-have in your toolkit.

> *"Your creative journey in the print-on-demand world is akin to painting on a vast digital canvas. These tools? Consider them your brushes, and AI is the wind beneath your wings, guiding each stroke. Dive in, experiment, and let your imagination soar."*

BONUS:

Everbee: Your Personalized Market Researcher and Design Assistant

Are you looking for a personal assistant who not only helps with design but also gives you valuable insights about market trends? Everbee does precisely that. Here's how you can use Everbee for your Etsy venture:

1. **Market Research Insights:** Before diving into any design process, understanding the market is crucial. Everbee's AI algorithms sift through vast amounts of data from multiple sources, presenting you with insights about best-selling products. It is a magnifying glass over the Etsy marketplace, revealing what's hot and what's not.

2. **Trend Forecasting:** Besides the present, Everbee also forecasts trends, giving you an edge over competitors. Being ahead in the print-on-demand game means tapping into future popular niches before they become saturated.

3. **Design Inspiration:** With market insights, it's time to create! Everbee suggests design inspirations based on the trends it's identified. No more shooting in the dark; align your creative process with the market's desires.

4. **Seamless Integration with Other Tools:** Everbee offers design insights, and tools like Canva and Midjourney can bring those insights to life. The synergy between market

research and actual design creation has never been this seamless.

PRO TIP:

Always keep an eye on the insights Everbee provides. Markets evolve, and what's trendy today might not be in a month. Let Everbee be your compass in the ever-shifting landscape of print-on-demand on Etsy.

Action Steps: Selling Print-on-Demand on Etsy

1. Research Your Niche
2. Open Your Etsy Shop
3. Create Your Brand
4. Choose a Print-on-Demand Provider
5. Designing Your Products
6. List Your Products on Etsy
7. Set Up Pricing and Payments
8. Determine Shipping Details
9. Marketing Your Products

Remember, as with all things, consistency is key. As you persistently refine and promote your shop, you'll learn more about what works best for your audience and your unique style. Best of luck with your print-on-demand venture on Etsy!

1. Researching Your Niche Using Everbee: A Beginner's Guide

1. Sign Up and Log In:

First, head over to the Everbee website.

If you're new, sign up for an account. If you already have one, simply log in.

2. Access the Market Research Dashboard:

Once logged in, look for a section called "Market Research" or something similar. It's where Everbee gathers data and trends for you.

3. Choose 'Etsy' as Your Preferred Platform:

Everbee offers insights for various platforms. Ensure you select 'Etsy' to get data tailored to this platform.

4. Begin with Broad Categories:

Start your research by looking at broad categories like "clothing", "home decor", or "jewelry".

This will give you a general idea of which types of products are trending on Etsy in your niche

5. Dive Deeper into Specifics:

Within each broad category, Everbee will show subcategories or themes. For instance, under "clothing", you might see subcategories like "vintage tees", "graphic hoodies", or "anime tank tops".

These subcategories give you a better idea of the specific product types people seek.

6. Check the Top-Selling Products:

Everbee provides a list showcasing top-selling products in each category or subcategory.

Pay attention to these! They provide inspiration and show the buyer's current interests.

7. Study Design Themes:

Not only do you want to know which products are popular,

but you'll also want to understand the popular designs and themes.

Are there certain colors, patterns, characters, or words that are trending? For instance, tropical themes may trend in the summer, or certain quotes are becoming popular.

8. Keep an Eye on Seasonal Trends:

Everbee highlights certain seasonal trends. For example, during the holidays, Christmas-themed designs might be trending.

This helps you plan your designs ahead of time and release them right when demand starts to peak.

9. Save Your Findings:

Make notes of your gathered information in a document. This will be your go-to resource as you design products for your Etsy shop.

10. Visit Regularly:

Trends change, and what's popular now might not be in a few months. Make it a habit to visit Everbee regularly, perhaps once a week or once a month, to stay updated on the latest trends and demands.

> *By following these steps, even a beginner can utilize Everbee and find the perfect niche for their Etsy print-on-demand shop. Remember, while data is a fantastic guide, always blend it with your unique creativity and style. Happy researching!*

2. Setting Up Your Etsy Shop

Ready to kickstart your entrepreneurial journey? If you are confused about setting up your Etsy shop, don't worry. I've got you covered. Let's break it down into bite-sized steps. Trust me, by the end of this, you'll wonder why you didn't start sooner!

1. Create an Account:

Go to Etsy.com.

Click on the "Sell on Etsy" button (usually found in the top right corner).

Click on the "Open Your Etsy Shop" button.

Choose your preferred language, country, and currency from the drop-down menus, then click 'Save and Continue'.

2. Shop Preferences:

Set your shop's primary language, country, and currency.

3. Name Your Shop:

Think of a unique and catchy name for your shop.

Enter the name in the "Shop Name" section. Make sure it's available. If not, try variations until you find one that is.

4. Stock Your Shop:

Click on 'Add a Listing' to start adding products.

Upload clear and high-quality photos of the product. Etsy recommends having several pictures from different angles.

Fill out the title, description, and other necessary details about the product.

Set a price for your product.

Determine how you'll ship the product, including shipping costs.

5. Choose a Payment Method:

Etsy provides several options, like Etsy Payments (buyers can pay in many ways, and you get the money in your bank), PayPal, etc. Choose the one that suits you best.

6. Set Up Billing:

Even though you'll be making money, Etsy does have some fees. You'll need to provide payment details (like a credit card) to cover any fees and charges.

7. Shop Settings:

Start from scratch. Open the project you named earlier, and all your brand elements will be ready to use.

> *The best part about RelayThat is that it does most of the heavy lifting for you. So, even if you're not a design genius, you'll make professional-looking designs in no time. Have fun, and let your creativity shine!*

3. Setting Up and Creating a Brand with RelayThat

1. Sign Up:

Visit the RelayThat website.

Click the "Get Started" or "Sign Up" button, usually located at the top right corner.

Enter your details or sign up with a social media account to create your account.

2. Dashboard Introduction:

Once logged in, you'll be taken to your dashboard. This is where all your projects will appear. It might be empty now, but not for long!

3. Start a New Project:

Click on the "Create a New Workspace" or similar button.

Name your project. Think of it as naming a folder where all designs related to one topic or brand will be stored.

4. Choose a Brand Style:

RelayThat will show you different layouts and styles.

Browse through them and choose one that you think suits your brand or idea the best.

5. Customize Your Brand Elements:

Logo: Upload your brand logo. If you don't have one, don't worry; you can always add or change this later.

Colors: Choose the main colors you want for your brand. Maybe your favorite color or something that represents what you're doing!

Fonts: Select the type of font that matches your brand's feel. Whether it's fun, serious, or creative, pick what feels right.

6. Add Content:

Images: RelayThat offers a library of images, or you can upload your own.

Text: Add titles, subtitles, or any other information you want to display on your designs.

7. Automatic Designs:

Once you add your content, RelayThat will automatically create designs for you based on the style you chose. It'll offer designs for social media, websites, banners, and more.

8. Review and Adjust:

Look through the designs. If something doesn't look right or you want to change it, simply click on the design and make your adjustments.

9. Save and Download:

When you're happy with a design, save it.

You can then download it to your computer or share it directly to your social media.

10. Reusing Your Brand Style:

The next time you want to create a design for the same brand, you don't have to start from scratch. Just open the project you named earlier, and all your brand elements will be ready to use.

> *Remember, the best part about RelayThat is that it does most of the heavy lifting for you. So even if you're not a design genius, you'll be making professional-looking designs in no time. Have fun and let your creativity shine!*

4. Choosing and Setting Up with Printify as Your Print-On-Demand Provider

1. Understanding Print-On-Demand:

It's like having a backstage pass to your own merchandise store. You're the designer; Printify is your stage crew. They handle printing and shipping while you focus on the fun stuff—creating!

Researching Providers:

A quick online search would show you many options, but for our guide, we've chosen Printify due to its userfriendly interface and wide range of product offerings.

Products They Offer:

Printify offers a wide range of products, from apparel to home decor. It's a playground for your creative designs.

Where Do They Ship?

Printify provides shipping to most parts of the world, but always double-check if they cover where your audience is.

Costs Involved:

The cost of every product varies. When pricing your product, it's crucial to factor in its cost and the margin you need to make a profit.

Let's Set Up an Account with Printify:

Visit Printify's official website.

Click on the "Start Selling" button at the top right corner.

You can sign up using your email or other platforms like Google or Apple. Choose the method that's most convenient for you.

If you choose email, provide the necessary details: your email address and a password.

Hit the "Sign Up" button.

Confirming Your Email:

Go to your email inbox and find the confirmation email from Printify.

Click on the confirmation link. This ensures your email is valid and keeps your account secure.

Exploring Your Printify Dashboard:

After logging in, you'll land on your dashboard. It's your mission control! Here, you'll manage products, see orders, and track your sales.

Familiarize yourself with the platform. Printify's userfriendly interface makes it easy, even for beginners.

Safety Measures:

Protect your account. Use a unique password and consider changing it occasionally.

Getting Assistance:

Printify has a detailed "Help Center". If you get stuck or have questions, they have numerous articles and guides.

Ready, Set, Design!

With your Printify account now set, you can upload designs, choose products, and start your online store's journey.

> *Every great store starts with the first product. With Printify, you've got a reliable partner to help bring your creative visions to life. Stay enthusiastic, keep learning, and soon enough, you'll see your designs loved by customers worldwide. As always, enjoy the journey!*

5. Design Your Product:

1. **Start Your Creative Engine:** Head over to Canva's website. If you don't have an account yet, you can sign up for free.

2. **Pick a Template:** On the homepage, you'll see a bunch of design types. For our purpose, search for something like a "t-shirt" or "poster", whichever fits your product type.

3. **Enter the Canvas:** Once you select a template, you'll be taken to the design canvas. Here's where the magic happens!

4. **Unleash Your Creativity:** On the left, you'll find a userfriendly panel with options like 'Elements', 'Text', and 'Uploads'. Click on 'Elements' to easily incorporate shapes, lines, or graphics into your project. If you want to add text, simply click 'Text' to access a variety of fonts and styles. This intuitive interface ensures a seamless creative process without any interruptions.

5. **Stay Unique:** Remember that research you did earlier? Use that to influence your designs. Maybe the market wants vintage cat posters or quirky coffee mug quotes. Let your research guide your creativity.

6. **Avoid Oops Moments:** Ensure you're not using copyrighted images or designs. Canva does offer a lot of free graphics, but always double-check.

7. **Download and Save:** Once satisfied with your masterpiece, click the 'Download' button on the top right. Choose the format you want (usually PNG for prints), and voilà! Your design is ready.

DESIGNING WITH MIDJOURNEY

1. **Embark on the Midjourney Adventure:** First, you'll want to visit Midjourney's platform.

2. **Create Your Discord Account:** To use Midjourney, you'll need to have a Discord account. If you don't have one, don't worry! Setting up a Discord account is a breeze. Just go to Discord's official website, click on 'Register', and follow the easy steps to create your account.

3. **Connect with Midjourney on Discord:** Once your Discord account is ready, find Midjourney's Discord community and join it. This will be your hub for all things Midjourney.

4. **Dive into Design:** On the Midjourney Discord, you'll find resources, guides, and tools to help you start your design

8

journey. There might be different channels or sections dedicated to various design topics; explore them!

5. **Harness the Potential of Keywords:** Midjourney has a cool inspiration feature. Enter a keyword related to your design, and it'll show related aesthetics to spark your creativity.

6. **No Copycats Allowed:** Always make sure your designs are unique. Using copyrighted or trademarked elements is a big no-no. Stay original; stay fresh!

7. **Export and Celebrate:** Once you're proud of your design, follow the steps to export it in the correct format. It is prepared to be displayed to the world on the product of your choice.

8. **Important Note:** You will need to sign up for their monthly subscription to use the images you create for commercial use.

Remember, every tool has its distinctive charm and strengths. Midjourney, with its tight-knit Discord community, provides not just a platform for design but also a space to share, learn, and grow. Designing should be fun, so enjoy the process and watch your creations come to life!

BONUS: PROMPTS TO IGNITE YOUR IMAGINATION!

Kickstart Your Imagination with Midjourney

When using Midjourney on Discord, the magic starts with the prompt //imagine. It's like the key to a treasure chest, opening up endless design possibilities. Here are some example prompts to get you started:

1. Nature-themed T-shirt Designs

Prompt: //imagine A serene mountain landscape with a setting sun for a t-shirt design

2. Mystical Phone Cases

Prompt: //imagine A phone case design with a dreamy unicorn under a starlit sky

3. Vintage-Style Poster

Prompt: //imagine A retro poster advertising a summer beach festival in the 1980s

4. Space-Inspired Coffee Mugs

Prompt: //imagine A coffee mug design featuring an astronaut sipping coffee on the moon

5. Whimsical Notebook Covers

Prompt: //imagine A notebook cover with a playful dragon guarding a castle of books

6. Funky Sock Patterns

Prompt: //imagine A pair of socks adorned with dancing pineapples and sunglasses.

Initiate your interaction with Midjourney using the //imagine prompt. The secret handshake lets the AI know you're ready to dive deep into the world of imagination. With every prompt, you're not just asking the tool to design for you; you're partnering with it to create something extraordinary. So, let your collaborative creativity run wild, and happy designing!

6. List Your Products on Etsy:

Step 1: Log Into Your Etsy Shop

If you haven't already created an Etsy shop, ensure you've done so. Once that's out of the way, log into your Etsy account and navigate to your shop's dashboard.

Step 2: Click the Golden Button

On your shop's dashboard, you'll see a button that says, "Add a new listing". Click on it. You're now on the path to showcasing your masterpiece to the world!

Step 3: Choose Your Category

Etsy will ask what you're selling. Is it a t-shirt? A mug? Maybe a trendy phone case? Pick the category that fits your product the best. This helps buyers find your cool stuff easily.

Step 4: Picture Time!

Now, you'll want to show everyone how awesome your product looks. Upload the mock-up images of your design on the product. This is like the window display at stores—it's what catches people's eyes! Make sure your photos are bright and clear. If possible, provide a 360-degree view of your product to show your customers the real deal.

Step 5: Name Your Creation

Give your product a catchy name. Think of something that makes people say, "I want that"!

Step 6: Describe with Style

Here's where you tell everyone about the cool thing you're selling. Write a clear description of your product. Tell them it's a 'print-on-demand' item so they know it's special and made just for them. Try to answer any questions they might have in this description, like sizes available, colors, or materials used.

Step 7: Set the Price

Decide how much money you want to make from selling this item. Consider the cost of making it, and add a bit extra for your hard work and creativity.

Step 8: Shipping Details

Let your buyers know how long it'll take for you to get the product ready to ship and how long the shipping might take. This is important, as everyone is always eager to get their hands on their new purchase.

Step 9: Complete the Listing

After filling out any remaining details, hit the "Publish" button. And voilà! Your product is now out in the Etsy universe, waiting for someone to fall in love with it.

Step 10: Celebrate!

You've just listed a product on Etsy! That's a big deal. Pat yourself on the back, do a little dance, and get ready for the world to see your creativity.

HERE'S A SECRET

> *Every product you add increases the chance of someone finding and loving your creations. So, keep designing, listing, and letting everyone see what you've got!*

7. Set Up Pricing and Payments on Etsy:

Step 1: Grab a Calculator

Before we start, make sure you have a calculator handy. It will help you crunch some numbers and set the right price.

Step 2: Understand Your Costs

First things first, find out how much the product costs to make. This includes:

The Blank Product: This is the plain T-shirt, mug, or whatever item you print your design on.

Printing Costs: This is what you pay to get your design printed on the product.

Add these two numbers together to get your total cost.

Step 3: Don't Forget Etsy's Share

Etsy charges a small fee for letting you use their platform. This might change, but as of my last update, it's 5% of the price plus a 3% payment processing fee. It sounds a bit tricky, but all you need to remember is to factor these fees into your price. You can look up an online Etsy fee calculator and use it to make this part super easy.

Step 4: Decide Your Profit

This is the fun part! Decide how much you want to earn from selling each item. This is called the profit margin. If your total cost is $10 and you want to make $5 for each sale, you'd set the selling price at $15 (plus Etsy's fees).

Step 5: Set Your Price on Etsy

Now, when creating or editing a product listing on Etsy, there's a box where you put in your price. Using your calculator, add together your total cost, Etsy's fees, and your profit margin. This is the number you'll put in that box.

Step 6: Choose How You Get Paid

Etsy wants to make sure you get your money! So, they offer different ways to receive payments:

Etsy Payments: This is super easy. Buyers can pay with credit cards, debit cards, and other methods, and the money will come to your bank account.

PayPal: A popular online wallet. If you have a PayPal account, you can receive money there.

Choose the method that feels right for you. Remember, however, that you'll need to set up accounts with these services (like PayPal) outside of Etsy. So, make sure you have that sorted, too.

Step 7: Activate Payment Methods on Etsy

In your Etsy dashboard, there's a section called Shop Manager. Click on that, then find Finances and then Payment Settings. Here, you can select and set up your chosen payment methods. Make sure to save your choices!

And just like that, you've set your prices and told Etsy how you'd like to get paid. Great job! Whenever you sell something, the money will go to your chosen payment method, and you'll be one step closer to buying that thing you've been saving up for!

8. Determine Shipping Details with Your Print-on-Demand Provider:

Shipping items may seem daunting for new Etsy sellers, but it doesn't need to be! To transport your awesome products from the factory to your customer's doorstep involves several crucial steps. Allow me to guide you through this process.

Step 1: Pick a Print-on-Demand Provider with Drop Shipping

Drop shipping sounds fancy, but it's just a way of sending products directly from where they're made to your customer without you touching anything. So, pick a provider (like Printify, Printful, or others) that offers this. They'll handle all the nitty-gritty shipping details for you!

Step 2: Integration Magic

Now, you need your print-on-demand provider connected to your Etsy shop. This way, when someone orders from your shop, the provider knows to start making and sending the product. Most of the time, these providers will have special tools or plugins that help connect everything together. Just follow the setup guides; it's usually super easy, with pictures and all!

Step 3: Set Up Shipping Profiles on Etsy

Head over to your Etsy dashboard and find the Shop Manager. Then click on Settings and select Shipping Settings. Here, you can create a shipping profile. This is just a fancy way of telling Etsy where you're sending your products from, how long it usually takes to get made, and how long it takes to reach your customers.

Step 4: Choose Shipping Costs

Many print-on-demand providers include the shipping cost in the price. But if they don't, they'll tell you how much it is. Similarly, you can add this cost to your product price or charge it separately. Either way, make sure it's clear to your customers.

Step 5: Automatic Updates

Once everything's set up, your print-on-demand provider should automatically update the tracking numbers and shipping information on Etsy when they send out an item. This means your customer will know where their package is and when it's arriving. Cool, right?

Step 6: Always Keep an Eye Out

Even though a lot of this is automatic, always cross-check once in a while to ensure everything is smooth sailing. And if a customer messages you about their order, you'll have all the information readily available.

And just like that, you've just set up shipping for your Etsy shop with your print-on-demand provider. It might seem like a lot at first, but once it's up and running, it will be a breeze. You've got this, and I'm cheering you on every step of the way!

9. Spread the Word about Your Awesome Products: A Kid's Guide to Marketing on Etsy

Okay, so you have set up your Etsy store and your designs look fantastic, but how do you actually get people to see them? Enter the world of marketing! Don't worry, it's not as complicated as it sounds. Let's break it down together.

Step 1: Share on Social Media

Instagram: Post pictures of your products; maybe

even create some cool stories showing them off! Don't forget to use hashtags that fit what you're selling. If you're selling space-themed t-shirts, use #SpaceTees or #GalaxyFashion.

Facebook: Create a page for your store, invite friends and family to like it, and post regularly. Maybe even ask your relatives to share your posts. More shares = more eyes on your products!

TikTok: Time for some fun! Create short, catchy videos showing off your products. Maybe even dance with them if you feel like it. TikTok loves fun and creative stuff!

Step 2: Boost with Etsy Ads

On your Etsy dashboard, you'll see a spot called 'Etsy Ads'. This is a fantastic way to give your products a little boost. It's like saying, "Hey, look at my stuff first!" Please be aware that utilizing this feature costs a bit of money.

Step 3: Team Up with Influencers

You know those people on social media who have a large number of followers and constantly recommend products? They're called influencers. Reach out to them and see if they'd like to show off your stuff. Maybe send them a freebie, and in return, they will talk about it on their page!

Step 4: Keep Engaging:

Whenever someone comments on your posts or asks questions, reply back! People love it when they get attention. Plus, it'll show others that you care about your customers.

And that's how you get the word out about your fantastic products. Marketing is just about sharing what you love with the world and finding fun ways to do it. Remember, every big journey starts with the first step (or post!). So, get out there and start sharing!

Brandon's Top Tips to Stay Fresh and Fabulous on Etsy!

Wrapping this chapter up with some final sparks of wisdom. Being on Etsy is like riding a fun roller coaster. There will be ups, downs, and loopy-loops! To make sure you're always on the upswing, here are some golden nuggets just for you:

1. Always Be Tweaking:

Your Etsy shop is like a living, breathing thing—it needs regular check-ups!

Check Your Stats: Every week (or day if you're a super keener!), dive into your Etsy shop's analytics. See what's selling, what's not, and where your visitors are coming from.

Stay Fresh: Your designs rocked last season, but trends change! Keep an eye out for what's hot and update your designs to stay in vogue. Your customers will love the fresh vibes!

Adapt and Overcome: If a marketing strategy isn't working, don't be afraid to switch things up. Always be on the lookout for new ways to shine. Trial and error is the best way to learn.

2. Stay Hungry; Stay Updated

The world of print-on-demand and design is evolving at warp speed.

Keep learning: Make it a habit to follow design and e-commerce blogs or join online communities. Knowledge is power, after all!

Refresh Your Offerings: Think of your shop like your wardrobe. Every once in a while, out with the old and in with the new! Update your product offerings to keep your shop looking snazzy and current.

That's the tea, my friend! Dive in, have fun, and remember: In online selling, there's always something new to explore and learn. So keep that energy high, that spirit bright, and watch as your Etsy shop thrives and shines!

Hypothetical Example: Summer's Breakthrough in the Etsy Marketplace with AI

In the heart of Nashville, a young visionary named Summer found herself on the cusp of transformation. While the hum of country music formed the city's backdrop, Summer, with her radiant energy and an eye for design, stumbled upon the world of print-on-demand. The bustling marketplace of Etsy beckoned, and she decided to dive in.

Summer's initial days were filled with the excitement of setting up her Etsy shop. She had no formal training in design, but her heart resonated with the world of colors and patterns. That's when Canva became her closest ally. Its user-friendly interface allowed her to bring her visions to life on two of her chosen products: t-shirts and mugs.

Yet, Summer's creative spirit longed for something unique. While engaging with the online community on Discord, she stumbled upon Midjourney. Typing in the command //imagine, she asked the AI to envision a dreamy sunset by the beach. The AI's response became the touchstone for Summer's next series of designs. They weren't just graphics; they were fragments of dreams imprinted on everyday wear.

As her product range grew, she questioned herself: "What does the world want?" Everbee provided the answer. With its rich market insights, Summer discerned the trends and preferences of Etsy shoppers. Her Midjourney-inspired beach sunset design quickly became well-liked. Orders flowed in.

However, she didn't stop there. She turned social media into her stage, leveraging Instagram's picturesque platform and TikTok's engaging video format to showcase her designs effectively. The audience didn't just see products; they witnessed the birth of a brand.

Behind the scenes, Summer was more than just a designer. She became the heart and soul of her brand. Every customer query was met with enthusiasm, every review was cherished, and every piece of feedback looped back into improving her brand.

Today, as the sun sets in Nashville, it also rises on tote bags and phone cases worldwide, bearing Summer's signature design. It's not just a product; it's a piece of her journey, blending creativity, technology, and heart.

AI-Powered Print-on-Demand Success Checklist

🐝 Niche and Product Research

- ☐ Identify Your Target Audience.
- ☐ Use Everbee to Scout for Best-Selling Products and Trends.

🐝 Store Setup

- ☐ Establish Your Brand with Tools Like RelayThat.
- ☐ Choose a Reliable Print-on-Demand Provider (e.g., Printify).
- ☐ Set Up an Etsy Shop and Ensure Branding Consistency.

🐝 Design Creation

- ☐ Leverage Canva for Basic Designs.
- ☐ Use Midjourney on Discord to Get AI-Assisted Design Inspiration.
- ☐ Always Ensure Designs do not Infringe on Copyrights.

🐝 Listing Products on Etsy

- ☐ Upload High-Quality Mock-Up Images.
- ☐ Write Clear, Concise, and Appealing Product Descriptions.
- ☐ Specify that Products are Print-on-Demand.

Pricing and Payments

- ☐ Calculate Comprehensive Costs (Product, Printing, and Etsy Fees).
- ☐ Add Your Desired Profit Margin.
- ☐ Set Up Payment Methods on Etsy.

Shipping Details

- ☐ Confirm Your Provider's Drop-Shipping Capabilities.
- ☐ Ensure Smooth Integration
- ☐ Between Your Provider and Etsy for Automatic Shipping Detail Handling.

Marketing Mastery

- ☐ Share Your Listings on Popular Social Media Platforms.
- ☐ Invest in Etsy Ads for Intra-Platform Promotion.
- ☐ Collaborate with Influencers or Bloggers for Additional Exposure.

Customer Engagement

- ☐ Promptly Respond to Customer Queries.
- ☐ Foster a Positive Shopping Experience to Encourage Rave Reviews.

Continuous Optimization

- ☐ Regularly Review and Refresh Designs Based on Trends and Sales Data.
- ☐ Adjust Marketing Strategies as Needed.

Stay Updated

- ☐ Keep Abreast of Print-on-Demand and Design Industry Trends.
- ☐ Periodically Update Product Offerings.

> *Remember, while AI tools can power up your process, your unique creativity and dedication will set your store apart. Here's to your success in the AI-powered print-on-demand world!*

"Entrepreneurship is not just about building a business; it's about crafting a legacy that stands the test of time."

- Anonymous

CHAPTER 2

SELF-PUBLISHING MAGIC: SELLING BOOKS ON AMAZON KDP

> *"The best way to predict the future is to create it."*
>
> *-Peter Drucker*

T he self-publishing industry is booming. In 2022, self-published authors earned over $1.2 billion in royalties from Amazon KDP alone. This highlights self-publishing's power—authors can now publish without traditional publishers.

If you're an aspiring author, Amazon KDP is a great platform to start your self-publishing journey. It's free to join, and you can publish your book in eBook, paperback, and hardcover formats. Amazon also takes care of all the distribution and marketing for your book, so you can focus on writing and promoting your work.

Why is Self-Publishing the New Norm?

There are many reasons why self-publishing is becoming the new norm. Here are some of the most important ones:

Control:

When you self-publish, you have complete control over your book. You can choose the title, the cover, the price, and the marketing strategy. You also have complete control over your royalties.

The traditional publishing journey is like a slow stroll through a never-ending library, with manuscripts patiently waiting their turn to see the light of day. With self-publishing, authors have gained the ability to take their literary destinies into their own hands. They decide when and what to publish, retaining complete creative control over their works from writing to distribution.

Speed and Flexibility:

Self-publishing is much faster than traditional publishing. You can publish your book within weeks or even days, rather than waiting months or years for a conventional publisher to review and release it.

Authors can bring their books to market at a pace that suits their creative vision and objectives. This agility is especially relevant in today's fast-paced world, where trends evolve swiftly and timely relevance is the secret sauce for literary stardom

Cost:

Traditional publishing can be costly for authors. The average cost of traditional publishing is around $5,000 to $25,000. This includes the cost of editing, cover design, marketing, and distribution.

Self-publishing is much more affordable. The cost of self-publishing can vary depending on the services you choose to use. However, you can self-publish a book for as little as $100. This includes the cost of formatting your book, uploading it to a distributor, and creating a cover. Amazon offers a free publishing model; however, there are some external costs associated with self-publishing, such as:

Formatting: You must format your book to be ready for publication. This includes setting the margins, font size, and line spacing. You can do this yourself or hire a professional formatter.

Cover Design: You will need to create a cover for your book that is both attractive and eye-catching. You can do this yourself or hire a professional designer.

Marketing: You will need to market your book to potential readers. This can be done through online and offline channels, such as social media, book signings, and advertising.

Hence, self-publishing may seem expensive, discouraging some authors from pursuing it. However, there are many ways to save money on self-publishing. For example, you can do the formatting and cover design and use free or low-cost marketing tools.

Lucrative Royalties and Revenue:

Much like many aspects of life, money plays a significant role in the rise of self-publishing. Do you know what's incredible about self publishing compared to those old-school publishing deals? With self-publishing, authors keep way more of the cash they rake in from book sales. In contrast to traditional publishing contracts, which frequently provide authors with modest royalties, self-publishing offers a more lucrative revenue model, resulting in greater financial rewards. This can particularly appeal to writers who want to make a sustainable living from their literary endeavors.

Here are some specific examples of how self-publishing can lead to more lucrative royalties and revenue:

Traditional publishers typically offer authors royalties of 10% to 12% of the retail price of a book. Self-published authors, on the other hand, can earn royalties of up to 70%. That's a substantial jump!

Traditional publishers often require authors to pay for editing, cover design, and marketing costs. Self-published authors can save money on these costs by doing them themselves or hiring freelancers, cutting down the costs to nearly zero

Traditional publishers typically have a lengthy approval process for new books. This can mean waiting months or even years before your book is published. Self-published authors can publish their books much faster, often within weeks or even days. Staying motivated is all about keeping those quick wins rolling in!

When it comes to self-publishing, it's not all about the money. Two other factors bring colossal rewards, i.e.:

Reach:

With self-publishing, you can reach a global audience. People all over the world can read your book, which can be sold on Amazon and other online retailers.

Success:

Self-published authors are now more successful than ever before. Many self-published authors have achieved bestseller status, and some have even earned more money than traditionally published authors.

Challenges and Limitations of Self-Publishing:

While self-publishing has emerged as a transformative force in the literary world, it's important to acknowledge that it comes with its own challenges and limitations.

Quality Control: One of the most prominent challenges is maintaining consistent quality. The absence of traditional gatekeepers means that works of varying craftsmanship and professionalism flood the market. Ensuring your self-published book meets industry standards and stands out for its excellence is a significant challenge.

Visibility and Marketing: Self-published authors often struggle with getting their books noticed amidst the vast sea of content available. Traditional publishing houses have established marketing and distribution networks, while self-published authors need to invest time and effort into building their brand and promoting their work effectively.

Stigma: Despite the growing acceptance of self-published works, there can still be a lingering stigma associated with them. Some readers might assume that self-published books are of lower quality compared to traditionally published ones, making it essential to overcome this perception through impeccable presentation and storytelling.

Resource Investment: Self-publishing requires authors to wear multiple hats, from writing and editing to cover design and marketing. This demands a significant investment of time, effort, and sometimes finances, which can be daunting, especially for authors new to the publishing process.

Distribution Challenges: While platforms like Amazon KDP provide global reach, distribution beyond digital formats and online retailers can be limited. Getting self-published books into physical bookstores can be challenging without the support of a traditional publishing infrastructure.

In the face of these challenges, integrating AI tools into the self publishing process has emerged as a powerful solution. These tools offer an array of capabilities that conquer the many hurdles that authors may encounter. For example, AI-driven grammar and style checkers ensure that your writing is polished and errorfree, mitigating concerns about the quality of your work. Advanced AI algorithms can analyze market trends and reader preferences, guiding your marketing efforts for optimal visibility and engagement. Furthermore, AI-powered cover design and formatting tools assist in creating professional, eye-catching book layouts that enhance your book's appeal.

AI's data-driven insights can also aid in refining your book's content and targeting specific readerships, boosting your chances of resonating with your intended audience. In essence, AI becomes an invaluable ally in your self-publishing journey, offering the expertise and support that authors traditionally received from publishing houses.

In the next section, we will explore a range of AI tools and technologies that can be seamlessly utilized in your self-publishing process. These tools not only streamline the journey but also empower you to overcome challenges and present your work with the professionalism and quality that it deserves. Now, isn't that something?

The Role of AI: From Content Creation to Design

Thanks to artificial intelligence (AI), mundane tasks are becoming a thing of the past. AI is rapidly transforming the content creation and design industries. AI-powered tools are being used to automate tasks, generate creative content, and improve the quality of designs.

Here are some specific examples of how AI is being used in content creation and design:

Content Creation: AI-powered tools such as Bard, a language model from Google AI, can generate text, translate languages, write different kinds of creative content, and answer your questions in an informative way.

Design: AI-powered tools such as Adobe Sensei can be used to design websites, logos, and other visual content. They can analyze design elements and suggest improvements can also generate personalized designs based on user preferences.

Tools Spotlight: ChatGPT and Google Bard for Content Creation, AI Illustration Tools for Design

Trust me when I tell you these tools are the absolute G.O.A.T in selfpublishing. And I'm not just blowing smoke here. The list of tools I have compiled here is the result of extensive research and hands-on experience.

I've compiled a diverse array of tools that can significantly boost your self-publishing endeavors. In the following list, you will find various resources to assist you at every stage of your self-publishing journey, from content creation to marketing.

CONTENT GENERATION TOOLS

1. ChatGPT-4:

What it's for: ChatGPT-4 is a versatile AI model designed for natural language understanding and generation. It can be used for a wide range of content writing tasks, from drafting articles and blog posts to answering questions and generating creative text.

How it works: ChatGPT-4 uses a deep neural network trained on a vast amount of text data to generate humanlike responses. It relies on patterns and context in the input to generate coherent and contextually relevant text.

2. Bard:

What it's for: Bard is an AI content generation tool tailored explicitly for creative writing tasks, such as generating poetry, storytelling, or creative essays.

How it works: Bard uses a combination of language models and deep learning techniques to generate creative and imaginative text. It is trained on a diverse dataset of literary works to capture various styles and tones.

3. Claude:

What it's for: Claude is an AI tool for generating marketing and advertising content. It can help create compelling product descriptions, advertisements, and promotional materials.

How it works: Claude utilizes natural language processing and machine learning algorithms to understand the key features and benefits of a product. It then generates persuasive and engaging marketing copy based on this analysis.

4. CopyAI:

What it's for: CopyAI is a content generation tool that focuses on creating marketing copy, including ad headlines, product descriptions, and website content.

How it works: CopyAI uses a combination of pretrained language models and user prompts to generate persuasive and conversion-oriented copy. It allows users to input details about their product or service and tailors the content accordingly.

5. Writesonic:

What it's for: Writesonic is a content writing tool that assists with various writing tasks, including blog post outlines, product descriptions, and email content.

How it works: Writesonic uses AI to generate content based on user input and prompts. It can generate content in different styles and tones, making it a versatile tool for various writing needs.

6. Wordtune:

What it's for: Wordtune is an AI-powered writing assistant that helps users improve the clarity, style, and tone of their written content.

How it works: Wordtune analyzes the user's text and suggests rewriting sentences and phrases to enhance readability and overall quality. It provides real-time feedback to help users refine their writing.

Why Do I Use Both ChatGPT-4 and Google Bard?

I recommend using ChatGPT-4 and Google Bard parallel to each other. You will notice that there are times when Bard's response is more precise and to the point compared to ChatGPT-4, and vice versa. Here are some core reasons I recommend using both tools for content generation:

Diverse Perspectives: ChatGPT-4 and Google Bard have distinct strengths. ChatGPT-4 is proficient in factual and technical content, while Google Bard excels in creative and imaginative writing. Combining both ensures a wellrounded and engaging narrative.

Quality and Creativity: ChatGPT-4 provides a strong foundation with coherent and structured content. Google Bard adds creativity and flair, making the text more engaging for readers.

Efficiency: By utilizing both AI models, you can expedite the writing process. ChatGPT-4 can generate content quickly, and Google Bard can inject creativity, reducing the time required for revisions.

Content Variety: Different sections of your book may require various writing styles. Using both AI models helps adapt the style for each section's needs.

TIP

> *To create a unique voice, combining AI-generated content with your insights and experiences ensures that your book maintains authenticity.*

AI Illustration Tools for Design

1. DALL-E 3:

What it's for: OpenAI developed the text-to-image diffusion model known as DALL-E 3. It can be used to create realistic images from text descriptions.

How it works: You input a textual description, and DALL-E 3 generates an image that corresponds to the description. The model leverages a vast dataset of textimage pairs to create these illustrations. For example, you can type in "a cat riding a unicycle", and DALL-E 3 will generate a realistic image of a cat riding a unicycle. Try this right now!

2. NightCafe Creator:

What it's for: NightCafe developed NightCafe Creator, an AI art generator. It can be used to create various types of art, including paintings, drawings, and sculptures.

How it works: You can provide NightCafe Creator with a text prompt, an image, or even a song, and it will generate art based on your input. How cool is that?

3. DeepDream Generator:

What it's for: DeepDream Generator is also an AI art generator that uses neural networks to create dream-like images.

How it works: You can give the DeepDream Generator an image, and it will produce a brand-new image that is based on the input image but has undergone neural network transformation.

4. Adobe Firefly:

What it's for: Adobe Firefly is an AI-powered creative tool designed to unlock your imagination. It allows users to create stunning images, transform text, play with colors, and more, all using simple text prompts. Firefly offers a range of creative capabilities, including text-to-image generation, generative fill for object manipulation, applying text effects, generating color variations for vector artwork, creating images from interactive 3D elements, and easily extending image aspect ratios.

How it works: Adobe Firefly operates based on the input of text prompts in over 100 languages. Here's a breakdown of its key functions:

» **Text to Image:** Firefly can generate images based on detailed text descriptions. By describing the image you want in text, Firefly uses its generative AI capabilities to bring that description to life as an image.

» **Generative Fill:** Users can employ a brush tool to remove objects from an image or add new elements by simply painting them in. This feature enables creative visual content manipulation.

» **Text Effects:** Firefly enables the application of styles and textures to words and phrases, giving text a visually appealing and artistic touch.

» **Generative Recolor:** This feature generates various color variations for vector artwork. It allows users to explore different color schemes for their designs.

» **3D to Image:** Users can create images by interactively positioning 3D elements. This is particularly useful for those working with threedimensional graphics.

» **Extend Image:** Firefly simplifies changing the aspect ratio of an image with a single click. This can be handy for adapting visuals to different platforms and screen sizes.

1. Bing Create:

What is it for: Bing Create is a tool that can be used to generate images from text descriptions.

How does it work: Bing Create uses a generative AI system to create images from text descriptions. The system is trained on a massive dataset of images and text and learns the patterns and nuances of these different types of content. When you provide Bing Create with a text description, the system will generate a variety of other options, and you can choose the one that you like the best.

As discussed in the previous chapter, Canva is a general editing tool. Once you generate the art, the next step will be to edit and finalize it in Canva.

Action Steps: From Manuscript to Publishing with AI's Touch

1. Creating Accounts on Content Generation Platforms
2. Topic Research and Outline Building
3. Book Write-up
4. Working with Kindle Create
5. Prepare Cover Art using AI
6. Self-Publishing on Amazon KDP

1. Getting Started and Creating Accounts on Content Generation Platforms

Creating an OpenAI account and getting ChatGPT-4 is a piece of cake. Just sign up, choose the premium ChatGPT-4, and start using it for content ideas, outlines, and writing. Here's a step-by-step guide:

Step 1: Visit the OpenAI Website

Go to the OpenAI website at https://www.openai.com/.

Step 2: Sign Up or Log In

If you already have an OpenAI account, log in with your credentials. If not, click the "Sign Up" or "Get Started" button to create a new account.

Step 3: Provide Your Details

Fill in the required information to create your account. This typically includes your name, email address, and password. Ensure you use a secure password and save it for future reference.

Step 4: Verify Your Email

After providing your details, OpenAI will send a verification link to the email address you provided. Go to your email inbox, find the email from OpenAI, and click the verification link to confirm your email address.

Step 5: Set Up Your Account

Follow the on-screen instructions to complete your account setup. This may include adding additional information or preferences.

Step 6: Access ChatGPT

Once your account is set up and verified, you can access ChatGPT-3.5. You may be directed to a dashboard where you can manage your usage and access different services.

Step 7: Purchase ChatGPT-4

To use ChatGPT-4, you'll need to purchase a subscription.

On your dashboard, look for options related to subscriptions or pricing. It may be labeled "Upgrade" or "Get Premium".

There is only one option at the moment, i.e., $20 for a month.

Review the pricing details and click the "Subscribe" or "Purchase" button.

Step 8: Payment

Provide your payment details to complete the subscription process. Ensure that your payment information is accurate and up-to-date.

Step 9: Confirmation

Once your payment is processed successfully, you should receive a confirmation message. Your ChatGPT-4 subscription is now active.

Step 10: Access ChatGPT-4

Return to your dashboard or main account page. Now, you can use ChatGPT-4 alongside the free ChatGPT-3.5 while creating content.

Top Tips to Tweak Content Generation Platforms for Book Creation

Seldom people are aware of this, but what I'm sharing here is the influence of custom instructions on the performance, which helps it generate more accurate and relevant content. These instructions can include the following:

Tone: The text's tone, such as formal, informal, or humorous.

Style: The style of the text, such as academic, business, or creative.

Length: The length of the text, such as short, medium, or long.

Specific details: Any specific details that you want the text to include.

You can also provide feedback on the results that you get to help ChatGPT learn and improve its performance.

Here are some examples of custom instructions that you can use:

Generate a short, informal text about the benefits of using xx products.

Generate a medium-length, academic text about the history of artificial intelligence.

Generate a long, creative text about a future where artificial intelligence is used to solve global problems.

> *Custom instructions are the wizard's wand of AI content creation. They are helping you leverage AI content writing platforms to generate high-quality content tailored to your need*

Google Bard

Here is a detailed guideline on how to create a Google Bard account and get started with your book-writing journey. This includes personalization, options for tweaking and generating high-quality text

Go to the Google Bard website: https://bard.google.com/ and click the "Sign Up" button.

If you have a Google account, you can use that to sign up. Or click the "Sign Up" button to create one.

Click on the "Create Account" button.

You will receive an email from Google Bard with a confirmation link. Click on the link to verify your account.

Once your account is verified, you can log in to the Google Bard dashboard.

To get started with book writing, you can use Google Bard to:

Generate ideas for your book: Google Bard can help you generate ideas for your book by brainstorming topics, characters, and plots.

Outline your book: Google Bard can help you outline your book by generating a list of chapters and scenes.

Write your book: Google Bard can help you write your book by generating text, translating languages, writing different kinds of creative content, and answering your questions in an informative way.

Top Tips for Google Bard

Based on my experience here, Google Bard excels over ChatGPT-4 in the following ways:

Access to More Data: Google Bard is trained on a massive dataset of text and code and can generate more accurate and relevant text.

Better Understanding of Context: Google Bard is better at understanding the context of a conversation, which generates more relevant and coherent text.

More Creative Capabilities: Google Bard is better at generating creative text formats, such as books, poems, code, scripts, musical pieces, email, letters, etc.

Ability to Access and Process Information from the Real World: Google Bard has access to and can process information from the real world through Google Search. Generate more up-to-date and accurate text.

Ability to Learn and Improve over Time: Google Bard is constantly learning and improving, which means that it will become better at generating text over time.

2. Topic Research and outline building

Use ChatGPT-4 to generate a list of potential book topics.

For example, you want to write a book on personal development. First, narrow down the topic. Ask ChatGPT by giving this prompt: "Narrow down the broad topic 'personal development' into niche categories" and click the send message icon.

You can further narrow down or pick a topic from the suggested list.

Once you have a list of topics, ask ChatGPT-4 to generate a list of potential book topics based on your interests.

ChatGPT-4 will then generate a list of potential book topics.

Digging Deeper into the Topic Research

Every great book begins with a spark of inspiration, but it takes hard work and research to turn that spark into a raging inferno. When considering writing a book on a specific topic, it's crucial to conduct thorough research beforehand. This ensures that your chosen subject has the potential to resonate with your target audience and achieve commercial success.

Are you wondering if your book idea is worth all the time and money it will take to write and publish? You're not alone. Many authors question themselves similarly, especially with Amazon becoming increasingly crowded. Some believe you need to be famous or have a following before succeeding in self-publishing.

Gone are the days of uncertainty when gauging the potential success of your book on Amazon. Today, authors have access to a wealth of critical data, analytics, and tools that can effectively assess the viability of their book idea before they even start writing.

You need to confirm three things to make sure your book idea has a good chance of reaching your target audience:

Is there a demand for your book idea? This means that people are actively looking for information on the topic you're writing about.

You can find this out by doing keyword research and looking at the search volume for related terms.

Are people willing to pay for your book? This means checking whether there is a market for your book and whether people are willing to spend money to learn more about the topic. You can find this out by looking at the prices of similar books and considering the value that your book will offer readers.

Is there too much competition? Do your research to validate if there are already a lot of books on the market that cover the same topic. If there is too much competition, it will be more difficult for your book to stand out. You can find this out by looking at the number of books that have been published on the topic and the reviews that they have received.

How to Learn if Your Book Idea Will Make Money

Once you've found an idea that people are interested in, you need to figure out if it's a moneymaker. Here are the steps involved:

Find the Amazon Best Seller Rank (ABSR) for the top 14 books on your topic. You can search for your idea or phrase in the Kindle store.

Use a Kindle sales calculator to convert the ABSRs into books sold per day. You can find a free calculator online.

Multiply the number of books sold per day by the sales price to get the gross daily revenue.

Multiply the gross figure by 0.7 (if each book is priced between $2.99 and $9.99) or by 0.3 if it's sold for any other amount. This gives the actual author's earnings after Amazon takes their cut.

Add all the daily author earnings figures together and divide by the number of books you've calculated for. This will give you an average daily earnings figure.

If the average daily earnings figure is an amount you'd be happy to earn, then your book idea has the potential to be profitable. You can also compare this figure to other book ideas to determine what is more profitable.

How to Determine if There's Room for Competition

Once you've determined that your book idea has the potential to be profitable, you need to figure out if there's enough demand for it. Here are some things to consider:

How many results appear in the Kindle store for your idea or phrase?

What is the ABSR for the top book?

What is the average ABSR for the top 3 book results?

What is the average ABSR for the top 14 book results?

The lower the ABSRs, the less competition there is. If there is a lot of competition, it will be more difficult to get your book noticed.

Finding the Right Balance

The ideal book idea has enough interest but not too much competition. This will give you the best chance of being successful.

Creating an Outline of a Book Using ChatGPT

Request for an Outline: Ask ChatGPT-4 to outline your content. You can specify the structure you have in mind, such as main headings and subheadings. For instance: "Generate an outline for an article on sustainable gardening with sections on 'Introduction', 'Benefits of Sustainable Gardening', and 'Practical Tips".

Pro Tip 1: Clarity in Structure: Be clear in your instructions regarding your desired structure. Specify the number of sections or chapters and the key points to cover in each.

Initiate Research

Submit your prompt, and ChatGPT-4 will begin the research process. It will provide an outline and relevant information based on your instructions.

Pro Tip 2: Evaluate Initial Output: Carefully review the initial outline and research findings provided by ChatGPT-4. Ensure that it aligns with your objective and contains relevant information.

Refine and Expand: Based on the initial output, refine and expand the outline as needed. You can ask ChatGPT-4 for more details on specific sections or request additional sub-points.

Pro Tip 3: Iterative Process: Consider this as an iterative process. Generate the initial outline, review it, and refine your instructions for further research and expansion.

Once the outlines are created, copy them into Google documents or other word-processing software.

Things to Avoid

Avoid vague or overly broad prompts. Specificity is key to getting relevant results.

Don't rely solely on AI-generated research. Always crossreference information from trusted sources.

Avoid plagiarism. Ensure that any information gathered from the AI is appropriately cited and attributed.

Human Touch

Finally, remember that while ChatGPT-4 can assist with research and outlining, it's important to add your unique insights, expertise, and a human touch to the content during the writing phase. AI can assist, but it's not a substitute for your expertise.

3. Book Write-up

Here comes the process of writing the book. The outline is ready, and major and minor headings are ready. Now, it's time to use the power of AI prompting to craft a factually accurate and captivating book that will be ready to hit the shelves.

Book write-up using outlines generated by ChatGPT-4 in conjunction with Google Bard can be a powerful combination for producing high-quality content. Here's a step-by-step process to highlight the importance of using both tools:

Step 1: Divide the Content: Divide your book into manageable sections or chapters based on your outlines.

This will help you focus on one segment at a time.

Step 2: Decide on Content Prompts: For each section, create specific content prompts for both ChatGPT-4 and Google Bard. These prompts should be clear and tailored to the content you need.

Step 3: ChatGPT-4 Writing: Submit the content prompts to ChatGPT-4. The AI can generate text quickly and is proficient in various writing styles. Review the output from ChatGPT-4. Ensure it aligns with your book's style and message. Edit and refine the content as needed. Add your insights, examples, and personal touch to make it unique and coherent. Copy the generated content to Google Docs or other word-processing software.

Step 4: Google Bard Writing: Use the content prompts you prepared for Google Bard. This AI excels at creative writing and can provide engaging and imaginative text.

Review the output from Google Bard. It can offer a different perspective or creative flair to your content. Edit and blend Google

Bard's content with the ChatGPT-4 content. This combination can create a rich and diverse narrative.

Step 5: Maintain Consistency: Ensure consistency in style and tone throughout your book. To maintain a unified voice, adjust and harmonize the content that both AI models produce.

Step 6: Fact-Checking and Research: While AI can provide valuable insights, remember to fact-check and conduct additional research when necessary to ensure accuracy and credibility.

Step 7: Final Review and Editing: Thoroughly review and edit the entire manuscript. Focus on structure, flow, and coherence. Add any personal anecdotes, experiences, or insights that make the content uniquely yours.

> *Keep writing and saving the file in Google Documents*
> *or other word-processing software.*

4. Working with Kindle Create

Kindle Create is a user-friendly software tool Amazon developed to simplify the eBook formatting process for authors and publishers. It's an essential tool for anyone looking to self-publish eBooks on Amazon Kindle Direct Publishing (KDP) and offers several benefits for authors:

How Authors Can Benefit from Kindle Create:

Easy Formatting: Kindle Create eliminates the need for authors to manually format their eBooks, which can be complex and time-consuming. Instead, it offers an intuitive interface where authors can import their manuscript and format it effortlessly.

Compatibility: eBooks formatted with Kindle Create are optimized for Kindle devices and apps. This ensures readers have a seamless and enjoyable reading experience, with well-formatted text and proper page breaks.

Enhanced eBook Features: Kindle Create allows authors to add features like drop caps, images, and chapter titles, enhancing the overall design of the eBook. These features can make the reading experience more visually appealing.

Preview Mode: Authors can use the built-in preview mode to see how their eBook will appear on various Kindle devices and apps. This helps authors catch and correct formatting issues before publishing.

Automatic Table of Contents: Kindle Create generates a table of contents automatically based on your manuscript's formatting, saving you the trouble of creating one manually.

Ease of Publishing: Once your eBook is formatted using Kindle Create, you can easily publish it directly to Amazon KDP from the tool. This streamlines the publishing process and reduces the likelihood of formatting errors during the upload.

Free Tool: Kindle Create is entirely free to download and use. There are no hidden fees or charges, making it a cost-effective solution for self-published authors

.Regular Updates: Amazon continually updates

Kindle Create to improve its functionality and address user feedback. Authors can expect ongoing support and enhancements to the tool.

Downloading and Installing the Software

Here's a step-by-step guide to downloading and installing Kindle Create, Amazon's eBook formatting tool:

1. Access the Kindle Create Download Page

Open your web browser and go to the official Kindle Create download page on Amazon's website.

2. Choose Your Operating System

On the Kindle Create download page, you'll see two options for operating systems: Windows and macOS. Select the version that matches your computer's operating system.

3. Download Kindle Create

Click the "Download for [Your Operating System]" button. This will initiate the download process. Depending on your browser settings, you may be prompted to confirm the download or select a location to save the installation file.

4. Locate the Downloaded File

Once the download is complete, locate the installation file on your computer. By default, it's often found in your computer's "Downloads" folder, but you can choose a different location during the download process.

5. Run the Installer

Double-click the installation file to run the Kindle Create installer. Follow the on-screen instructions to begin the installation process.

6. Accept the License Agreement.

During the installation, you'll be presented with Amazon's License Agreement. Carefully read through the agreement, and if you agree to the terms, click the "Accept" or "Agree" button to proceed.

7. Choose the Installation Location.

You'll be prompted to choose the installation location for Kindle Create. The default location is usually the "Program Files" folder on Windows or the "Applications" folder on macOS. You can change this location if needed.

8. Begin Installation

Click the "Install" or "Start Installation" button to begin the installation process. Kindle Create will be installed on your computer. Wait for the installation to complete. Once it's finished, you'll typically see a confirmation message indicating that Kindle Create has been successfully installed.

9. Launch Kindle Create

After installation, you can launch Kindle Create by locating its shortcut icon on your desktop (Windows) or Applications folder (MacOS). Double-click the icon to open the program.

10. Sign In (Optional)

If prompted, you can sign in to your Amazon account within Kindle Create. This step is optional but may be required if you publish your eBooks directly to Amazon KDP from the tool.

> *That's it! It's as simple as that. You've successfully downloaded and installed Kindle Create on your computer. You can now use this tool to format and publish your eBooks on Amazon Kindle Direct Publishing.*

USING KINDLE CREATE

Here's a step-by-step guide on how to use Kindle Create to finalize your book. Let's talk about its features, how to use them, and also instructions on using templates:

1. Open Kindle Create

Launch the Kindle Create application on your computer by double-clicking its icon.

2. Open Your Manuscript

Click on "File" in the top left corner and select "Open Manuscript" from the drop-down menu.

Locate and select your manuscript file (usually in docx or kcb format) and click "Open."

3. Importing Your Manuscript

Kindle Create will automatically import your manuscript. It may take a moment, depending on your manuscript's length.

4. Explore Your Manuscript

You'll now see your manuscript divided into chapters or sections on the left-hand side of the interface. Use the table of contents to navigate through your book.

5. Formatting and Editing

Kindle Create provides various formatting and editing options:

Text Formatting: Select text in your manuscript and use the formatting options in the toolbar to adjust font size, style, alignment, and more.

Paragraph Styles: Apply different paragraph styles (e.g., normal, heading, subheading) to format your text consistently.

Images: You can insert pictures into your eBook. Use the "Insert" option in the toolbar to add images and adjust their placement within the text.

Page Breaks: Ensure proper page breaks between chapters or sections by selecting "Insert Page Break" from the toolbar.

6. Using Templates (Optional):

Kindle Create provides templates for various eBook types, such as novels, textbooks, and poetry. To use a template:

Click on "File" and select "New Manuscript from Template".

Choose a template that suits your book type and preferences.

Start writing your content within the template, which includes pre-set styles and formatting.

7. Enhance Your eBook

Kindle Create offers additional features to enhance your eBook:

Drop Caps: Add drop caps to the beginning of chapters for a visually appealing start.

Chapter Titles: Customize chapter titles and adjust their formatting.

Auto-Generated Table of Contents: Kindle Create can automatically create a table of contents based on your manuscript's formatting.

8. Review Your eBook

Regularly use the "Preview" button to review how your eBook will appear on various Kindle devices and apps. This helps you catch any formatting issues and ensure a smooth reading experience.

9. Save Your Work

Periodically save your progress by clicking "File" and selecting "Save Manuscript". Though it saves copies of your work automatically.

> *Your hard work is about to pay off. The next step is publishing your book, but before that, let me help you create a fantastic book cover that will attract readers.*

5. Prepare Cover Art

The cover art of a book is often the first interaction potential readers have with your work. It provides a glimpse into the untold worlds that lie within. Its design plays a pivotal role in` attracting readers' attention and conveying the book's essence, inviting them to step into an explored world.

Important Sections of a Book Cover:

When designing a book cover, several crucial elements should be considered:

Title: The title should be prominent and easily readable. Choose a font style and size that align with your book's genre and mood.

Author's Name: Place the author's name near the top or bottom of the cover, depending on the design aesthetics. Established authors often have their names prominently displayed.

Images/Illustrations: Include visual elements that convey the book's essence. This could be a central image, characters, or symbolic elements related to the plot.

Typography: Pay attention to font choices, colors, and layout. The typography should be legible and complementary to the overall design.

Genre Indicators: Use visual cues that signal the book's genre. For instance, thriller covers often incorporate suspenseful imagery, while romance covers may feature romantic scenes or couples.

Back Cover (Print Books): If you're publishing a print book, the back cover is valuable space. This is an excellent place to include a brief synopsis, author bio, and endorsements.

The cover art of your Amazon book is a critical aspect of its marketing and sales potential. It's the gateway to your story or content, and its design should align with your target audience's expectations and evoke intrigue. A unique and captivating cover can make your book more discoverable, enhance sales, and leave a lasting impression on readers.

CREATING COVER ART USING DALLE-3

Creating a book cover with DALL·E 3 and finalizing the design with Canva can create a unique and eye-catching cover. Here's a step-by-step guide to achieve this:

1. Access DALL·E 3

Go to the DALL·E 3's platform

Create an account by clicking "Get Started" on the top right corner of the webpage.

Fill in the necessary details to create the account. Once done, you will be redirected to DALL·E 3's simple dashboard, where you can input text prompts to create the book cover art.

2. Define Your Vision

Before starting, have a clear vision of what you want your book cover to convey. Consider the mood, theme, and key elements you want to include.

3. Generate Cover Concepts

Use DALL·E 3 to generate initial cover concepts. Provide text prompts or descriptions that encapsulate your book's essence. For example, "Fantasy novel cover with a mystical forest."

Review the generated images and select the ones that align with your vision.

If nothing attracts you, try another modified prompt that aligns with your vision.

4. Customize and Refine

Using Canva to Finalize the Book Cover Design Finalization

Access Canva

Go to Canva's website (www.canva.com) and log in to your Canva account. If you don't have one, you can sign up for free. Detailed instructions are provided in Chapter 1 on how to create an account and the basic functionalities of Canva.

Create a New Design

Click "Create a design" on Canva's homepage.

Choose the custom dimensions for your book cover. Usually, this will depend on the trim size of your book and the resolution requirements established by your publishing platform (like Amazon KDP).

Click "Create a new design".

5. Upload Your Customized Image

Click "Uploads" on the left-hand menu.

Upload the custom book cover image created with DALL·E 3.

6. Add Text and Elements

Use Canva's tools to add text, such as your book title, author name, and any other text elements you want on the cover.

Explore Canva's extensive library of design elements, including fonts, graphics, and illustrations. These can be used to enhance your book cover.

7. Fine-Tune the Design

Adjust the position, size, and style of text and elements to create a balanced and visually appealing composition.

Experiment with different fonts, colors, and layouts until you achieve the desired look.

8. Save Your Design

Once you're satisfied with your book cover design, click the "Download" button in the top right corner of the Canva interface.

Select the appropriate file format (e.g., PDF or PNG) and download the cover to your computer.

Uploading the Cover Image in Kindle Create

1. Open Kindle Create

Launch the Kindle Create application on your computer by double-clicking its icon.

2. Open Your Manuscript

Click on "File" in the top left corner and select "Open Manuscript" from the drop-down menu.

Locate and select your manuscript file (usually in .docx or .kcb format) and click "Open".

3. Access the Book Cover Section

In Kindle Create, the book cover is typically added in a separate section at the beginning of your manuscript. Look for the "Cover" tab in the left-hand menu. Click on it to access the cover section.

4. Insert Your Book Cover Image

In the cover section, you'll find a designated area to insert your book cover image. It's labeled as "Add Cover Image".

Click on this area to open a file dialog box.

5. Locate Your Book Cover Image

Browse your computer to locate the book cover image you created and saved.

Select the book cover image file and click "Open".

6. Adjust and Position the Image

Kindle Create may automatically fit the book cover image to the appropriate dimensions. However, you can click and drag to adjust the positioning of the image within the designated cover area.

7. Save Your Changes

Once you're satisfied with the placement of your book cover image, make sure to save your changes. Click "Save" or "Save Manuscript" in the top menu to save your manuscript with the book cover image included.

8. Review Your Manuscript

Scroll through your manuscript using the table of contents on the left to ensure that your book cover image appears at the beginning of your book.

Once your manuscript is complete and you're satisfied with the book cover placement and content, kudos! The next step is to publish your eBook on Amazon.

6. Self-Publishing on Amazon KDP

Now that everything's set, the next question is: How do you make your book available to the world? It's easy. All you need to do is create an Amazon KDP account and publish your book. Here's how you do it:

Creating an account on Amazon KDP

1. Go to the KDP Website

To begin the process, open your web browser and visit the KDP website. On the KDP homepage, look for and click the "Join KDP" button. This button initiates the account creation process.

2. Enter Your Information

You'll be prompted to provide some basic information to create your account. Start by entering your name, email, and password.

3. Agree to the Terms

Carefully read through Amazon's terms of service. Once you've reviewed and agreed to the terms, click the "Create Account" button again.

4. Verify Your Email Address

After clicking "Create Account", Amazon will send a verification email to the email address you provided during registration.

Check your email inbox for this verification message. Please open the email and click on the verification link within it. This step confirms that your email address is valid.

5. Log In to Your KDP Account

With your email address verified, return to the KDP website.

Use the email address and password you provided during registration to log in to your newly created KDP account.

6. Fill out Your Profile

After logging in, you'll have the opportunity to complete your profile information. This includes details such as your author name, address (for tax and payment purposes), and bank account information, which is necessary for receiving royalties from your book sales.

The Step We All Are Waiting for – Finally Publishing Your Book

1. Open Kindle Create and Sign In

Launch the Kindle Create application on your computer. If you haven't already, sign in to your Amazon account. This ensures your book will be associated with your KDP (Kindle Direct Publishing) account.

2. Click on the "Publish" Button

Once you're signed in, you'll find a "Publish" button in the Kindle Create interface. Click on this button to begin the publishing process.

3. Select "Kindle Direct Publishing"

After clicking "Publish", you'll be prompted to choose your publishing platform. Select "Kindle Direct Publishing" to proceed. This will link your Kindle Create project with your KDP account.

4. Create a New Publication

In Kindle Create, click on the "Create New Publication" button. This initiates the process of adding your book to the platform for publishing.

5. Enter Book Details

Fill in essential book details, including the title, author's name, and the book's language. Make sure this information matches the points you've provided on your KDP account.

6. Select the Book Format

Choose the book format that you're using for your manuscript. Kindle Create supports various formats, such as reflowable, print replica, and comics. Select the format that best suits your book.

7. Upload Your Book File

Click on the option to upload your book file. Locate your prepared manuscript file on your computer and select it for upload. Kindle Create will process the file to make it compatible with Kindle devices and apps.

8. Add Book Metadata

Provide additional metadata for your book. This includes the book description, keywords, and categories. This information helps readers discover your book on Amazon.

9. Set Book Price and Publication Date

Specify the price at which you want to sell your eBook on Amazon. You can also set a publication date if you wish to schedule the release of your book for a future date.

10. Publish Your Book

After ensuring that all book details, metadata, and pricing information are accurate, click the "Publish" button. Kindle Create will initiate the publishing process, making your eBook available for sale on Amazon.

> *And there you have it; with the helping hand of AI, you're on your way to becoming a published author! These steps guide you through using Kindle Create, simplifying the process of formatting and sharing your work with readers on the Kindle platform.*

Hypothetical Example: Mike's Meteoric Rise as an AI-assisted Author

Mike, a thirty-six year old professional with a background in marketing, has always harbored a deep passion for writing. From an early age, he excelled in English classes and often found solace in crafting short stories and essays. However, the demands of his corporate career limited his ability to pursue writing seriously. Nevertheless, his love for the written word remained undiminished.

Mike continued to write in his free time. He maintained a personal blog where he shared his thoughts on a wide range of topics, from technology to personal development. His articles began attracting a small but dedicated readership. As a result of this, Mike made the decision to take his writing more seriously.

He aspired to write a book, a dream he had held for years. However, the thought of dedicating countless hours to research and writing, only to face the uncertainties of traditional publishing, was daunting. This is where AI came to his rescue.

Mike learned about AI-powered writing assistance tools like ChatGPT-4 and Google Bard. These AI models promise to assist writers in generating content, conducting research, and even refining their writing style. Excited by the possibilities, Mike decided to give them a try.

Using ChatGPT-4, Mike generated a list of potential book topics. He narrowed down his interests and asked the AI for more specific ideas. The AI's ability to provide insights and suggest niche categories helped him focus his book idea.

Mike knew that a successful book idea required validation. He used AI to assess demand, willingness to pay, and competition for his chosen topic. The AI helped him analyze market data and reader preferences, ensuring he invested time wisely.

Once Mike settled on a topic, he asked ChatGPT-4 to generate an outline for his book. He provided clear instructions, specifying main headings and subheadings. The AI offered a structured outline that served as a solid foundation for his book.

With the outline in hand, Mike set out to write his book. Here, he utilized both ChatGPT-4 and Google Bard. He divided his book into sections based on the outline, creating content prompts for each. ChatGPT-4 helped him produce factual and informative content, while Google Bard added creativity and a unique flair to his writing.

Despite the AI's assistance, Mike understood the importance of thorough research and fact-checking. He used AI for initial information gathering but ensured all facts were accurate by crossreferencing multiple sources.

Mike polished his manuscript to make it shine. He ensured consistency in style and tone, added personal anecdotes, and refined the content to make it uniquely his own.

The use of AI-assisted writing is not a replacement for his creativity, but to enhance it. The AI models were valuable collaborators, helping him overcome hurdles like topic selection, research, and content generation. His book-writing process was more efficient and streamlined, allowing him to realize his dream without compromising quality.

Mike's book, enriched by AI assistance, became a bestseller on Amazon. It received praise for its well-researched content and engaging writing style. Mike's story of leveraging AI to fulfill his passion for writing resonated with many aspiring authors.

His journey from a corporate professional to a successful AI-assisted author illustrates the transformative power of AI in the writing world. With the right tools and a commitment to maintaining creativity and authenticity, he achieved meteoric success as an author, inspiring others to embark on their writing journeys with confidence and AI support.

Checklist for Aspiring AI-Powered Authors:

✿ Create Accounts

- ☐ Create an OpenAI (ChatGPT) Account for Content Creation.
- ☐ Create a Google Bard Account.

✿ Topic Research and Outline Building

- ☐ Generate Niche Topics
- ☐ Validate Book Idea
- ☐ Evaluate Profit Potential
- ☐ Assess Market Competition
- ☐ Balance Interest and Competition

✿ Book Write-up

- ☐ Divide Content
- ☐ Create Content Prompts
- ☐ Submit Prompts to ChatGPT-4.
- ☐ Review and Edit ChatGPT-4's Output for Style and Message.
- ☐ Add Personal Insights and Examples.
- ☐ Blend Google Bard's Content with ChatGPT-4's.
- ☐ Copy Generated Content to a Word Processing Tool.
- ☐ Fact-Checking and Research

Thoroughly Review and Edit the Entire Manuscript.

- ☐ Focus on Structure, Flow, and Coherence.
- ☐ Add Personal Anecdotes and Insights.
- ☐ Save the File in a Word Processing Tool.

Working with Kindle Create

- ☐ Download Kindle Create.
- ☐ Begin Installation.
- ☐ Launch Kindle Create.

Using Kindle Create:

- ☐ Import Your Manuscript.
- ☐ Formatting and Editing
- ☐ Using Templates (Optional)

Enhance Your eBook.

- ☐ Drop Caps.
- ☐ Chapter Titles.
- ☐ Auto-Generated Table of Contents.
- ☐ Review Your eBook.
- ☐ Save Your Work.

Prepare Cover Art (DALL·E 3, Bing Create, Canva)

- ☐ Define Your Vision: Determine the mood, theme, and key elements you want to convey on your book cover.
- ☐ Generate Cover Concepts with DALL·E 3.
- ☐ Customize and Refine with DALL·E 3.

Finalize the Design with Canva

- ☐ Access Canva and create a new design with custom dimensions for your book cover.
- ☐ Add Text and Elements: Use Canva tools to include text elements like the book title, author name, and graphics.
- ☐ Fine-tune the Design: Adjust text and elements for a balanced and appealing composition.

Adding the Cover Image to Kindle Create

- ☐ Access the Book Cover Section:
- ☐ Insert your Book Cover Image.
- ☐ Adjust and Position the Image.
- ☐ Save Your Changes in Kindle Create.
- ☐ Review Your Manuscript.

Self-Publishing on Amazon KDP

- ☐ Create an Amazon KDP Account.

❧Publishing Your Book

- ☐ Use Kindle Create and Select "Kindle Direct Publishing."
- ☐ Enter Book Details.
- ☐ Select the Book Format.
- ☐ Upload Your Book File.
- ☐ Set Book Price and Publication Date.

> "I'm convinced that about half of what separates the successful entrepreneurs from the non-successful ones is pure perseverance." - Steve Jobs

CHAPTER 3

DIGITAL MARKETING WITH AI INSIGHTS

"*Your work is going to fill a large part of your life, and the only way to be truly satisfied is to do what you believe is great work. And the only way to do great work is to love what you do.*" - Steve Jobs

The Ever-expanding Universe of Digital Marketing:

The digital age has revolutionized marketing in ways never before seen. Traditional approaches, though not obsolete, have had to make room for innovative strategies that can keep pace with the rapid changes in consumer behavior, technology, and the digital environment as a whole.

The digital marketing world is constantly evolving, with businesses needing to adapt their strategies constantly. Therefore, the digital marketing world offers various channels, platforms, and strategies to assist businesses in their growth. These include search engine optimization (SEO), content marketing, social media marketing, email marketing, pay-per-click (PPC) advertising, influencer marketing, and more. Navigating this expansive landscape can be both exhilarating and overwhelming for marketers.

One of the key challenges in digital marketing is staying ahead of the curve, being proactive rather than reactive, and understanding the ever-shifting preferences and behaviors of the target audience. This is where the fusion of digital marketing with artificial intelligence (AI) insights becomes a game-changer.

Benefits of AI in Predicting Trends and Optimizing Campaigns

AI has ushered in a new era of digital marketing, one characterized by data-driven decision-making, precision targeting, and unparalleled insights. And I'm here to tell you all about it. Here are some of the benefits of incorporating AI into your digital marketing strategy:

1. Predicting Trends

Advanced Data Analysis: AI tools can process vast amounts of data in real-time, identifying emerging trends, consumer sentiments, and market shifts that might go unnoticed by human analysts.

Anticipating Customer Behavior: AI algorithms can analyze historical customer data to predict future behavior. For instance, they can forecast which products will likely be in demand during specific seasons or events, enabling businesses to prepare accordingly.

2. Personalized Customer Experiences

Dynamic Content Creation: AI-driven content personalization ensures customers see content tailored to their preferences and interests, increasing engagement and conversion rates.

Product Recommendations: AI-powered recommendation engines analyze customer behavior and browsing history to suggest products or services that align with individual tastes, significantly boosting cross-selling and upselling opportunities.

3. Enhanced Customer Engagement

Chatbots and Virtual Assistants: Navigating customer conversations isn't always a breeze, and it can be a real-time drain. But thanks to AI, we've got a handy shortcut to smooth things out. AI-powered chatbots can engage with customers 24/7, answering queries, providing information, and even assisting in the sales process, enhancing user experience and satisfaction.

Segmentation and Targeting: AI algorithms help marketers divide audiences into groups based on different factors. They can create ads that are more personalized, resulting in improved click-through rates and conversion rates.

4. Improved Campaign Optimization

Real-Time Analytics: AI provides instant insights into the performance of marketing campaigns, allowing marketers to make data-driven adjustments on the fly to maximize ROI.

A/B Testing Automation: AI can streamline A/B testing processes, automatically optimizing ad creative, headlines, and other campaign elements to achieve better results.

5. Fraud Detection and Prevention

Ad Fraud Detection: On the internet, frauds is an unfortunate inevitability. However, AI stands guard as a vigilant sentinel, capable of identifying and flagging these deceitful activities in advertising, preventing budget wastage, and ensuring that marketing budgets are utilized efficiently.

6. SEO and Content Strategy

Keyword Research: AI tools can analyze search trends and competitor data to suggest the most effective keywords for SEO and content optimization.

Content Generation: AI-driven content generators assist in creating high-quality, relevant content at scale, saving time and resources.

> *Incorporating AI insights into your digital marketing strategy equips you with the tools to not only navigate the vast and dynamic digital landscape but also to thrive within it. As we delve deeper into this chapter, we will explore specific AI-driven techniques and tools that can empower marketers to harness the full potential of AI in achieving their digital marketing objectives. From predictive analytics to chatbots and beyond, the AI revolution in digital marketing is poised to reshape the way businesses connect with their audiences and foster growth in the digital era.*

Tools Spotlight: AI-driven Analytics and Ad Optimization Platforms

As the author of this book, I have personally conducted extensive research and hands-on exploration to compile the following list of cutting-edge tools for AI-driven analytics and ad optimization. These tools have been selected based on their proven capabilities to enhance marketing strategies, improve ad performance, and drive meaningful results in the dynamic digital environment.

Artificial intelligence (AI) has revolutionized how businesses collect, analyze, and use data. In digital marketing, AI is used to automate tasks, personalize experiences, and optimize campaigns. For example, AI can be used to:

Automatically collect and analyze data from various sources, such as website traffic, social media, and customer surveys.

Personalize marketing campaigns based on each customer's interests and needs.

Optimize campaigns for maximum results.

As a result of these capabilities, AI has the potential to revolutionize the way businesses operate and interact with their customers. For example, AI can be used to:

Improve customer service by providing personalized assistance and recommendations.

Develop new products and services that meet the needs of customers.

Let's look at the latest and most powerful AI tools for data analytics and ad optimization.

1. Adverity

What is Adverity?

Adverity is an AI-powered marketing data platform that helps businesses understand their marketing performance across channels and devices. It provides a single view of all marketing data across various channels and devices, combining online and offline data. With the use of AI, it identifies patterns and trends. This information can be used to enhance and optimize marketing campaigns, improve ROI, and make better business decisions.

How Does Adverity Work?

Adverity collects data from various sources, including Google Analytics, Facebook Ads, and Salesforce. It then uses AI to analyze this data and identify patterns and trends. This information is presented in a userfriendly dashboard that businesses can use to track their marketing performance and make better decisions.

Adverity's AI-powered Features Include:

Data Enrichment: Adverity enriches data by adding additional information, such as demographics, interests, and purchase history. This helps businesses to understand their customers better and target them more effectively.

Attribution Modeling: Adverity uses AI to model the impact of different marketing channels on sales and conversions. This helps businesses to understand which channels are most effective and allocate their budgets accordingly.

Campaign Optimization: Adverity uses AI to optimize marketing campaigns based on historical data and realtime insights. This helps businesses to improve the performance of their campaigns and achieve their goals.

Adverity's Benefits

Adverity offers several benefits for businesses, including:

Single View of Marketing Data: Adverity provides a single view of all marketing data, which makes it easier for businesses to track their performance and make better decisions.

AI-powered Insights: Adverity uses AI to identify patterns and trends in marketing data, which helps businesses understand their customers better and target them more effectively.

Campaign Optimization: Adverity uses AI to optimize marketing campaigns based on historical data and real-time insights, which helps businesses improve the

performance of their campaigns and achieve their goals.

Scalability: Adverity is scalable and can be used by businesses of all sizes.

2. Brand 24

What is Brand24?

Brand24 is a robust social listening tool designed to help individuals and businesses safeguard their online presence, monitor brand mentions, and gather crucial insights from public online conversations.

How Does Brand24 Work?

Social listening tools in marketing are absolutely mind-blowing! A few decades ago, instantly knowing what people say about your brand in real-time was unimaginable. But now, you can discover each time someone talks about your business, product, or service across the vast landscape of social media and the internet. Brand24 serves as a digital guardian, offering a wide range of capabilities to protect and enhance your online reputation:

Real-time Brand Monitoring: Brand24 enables tracking mentions of your brand, product, or chosen keywords across various online sources.

Crisis Prevention: Brand24 provides alerts for both positive and negative mentions, allowing you to respond promptly and manage your brand's reputation effectively.

Competitor Analysis: Gain a competitive edge by comparing your online presence, reach, and sentiment with your competitors.

Sentiment Analysis: Leverage AI-based sentiment analysis to categorize mentions positively, negatively, or neutral.

Influencer Identification: Discover influential authors and thought leaders in your industry—partner with them to amplify your brand's reach and credibility.

Advertising Value Equivalency: Quantify the value of your online mentions. Brand24 calculates the worth of your reach, helping you measure the impact of your online presence.

Brand24's Benefits:

Brand24's effectiveness is rooted in its intuitive interface and powerful features:

Keyword Setup: These could be your brand name, product name, or industry-specific terms.

Real-Time Monitoring: Brand24 continuously scans the web for mentions matching your specified keywords. It collects mentions from social media, blogs, news sites, forums, and more.

Alerts: Receive real-time alerts for new mentions, ensuring you're aware of any online activity related to your brand. Timely responses can defuse potential issues.

Hence, no more bad rep for your business.

Analysis and Reporting: Dive into detailed analytics beyond mere mention counting. Understand the reach, engagement, influence, and sentiment of your brand across various channels.

Exportable Reports: Create customizable reports summarizing your brand's online presence. These

reports can be used for internal analysis or shared with stakeholders.

Mobile and Desktop Access: Access your brand's data and alerts through a user-friendly mobile app or the desktop dashboard, ensuring you're connected wherever you are.

3. Surfer SEO

What is Surfer SEO?

Surfer SEO is an AI-powered SEO tool that helps businesses improve their search engine rankings. It provides insights into how search engines rank websites and helps companies to optimize their content accordingly.

How Does Surfer SEO Work?

Surfer SEO uses AI to analyze billions of search results and identify the factors that contribute to high rankings. This information is then used to create a personalized SEO audit for each website. The audit includes recommendations on how to improve the website's content, structure, and technical SEO.

Surfer SEO's AI-powered Features Include:

Keyword Research: Surfer SEO helps businesses find the right keywords to target. It provides insights into the search volume, competition, and difficulty of each keyword.

On-page Optimization: Surfer SEO provides recommendations on how to optimize website content for search engines. This includes tips on keyword usage, title tags, and meta descriptions.

Technical SEO: Surfer SEO helps businesses identify and fix technical SEO issues that could be affecting their rankings. This includes website code issues, loading speed, and security.

Content Analysis: Surfer SEO analyzes website content and identifies areas that could be improved. This includes tips on grammar, readability, and keyword usage.

Surfer SEO's Benefits:

Surfer SEO offers several benefits for businesses, including:

Improved Search Engine Rankings: Surfer SEO can help businesses improve their search engine rankings by providing insights into how search engines rank websites and assisting businesses to optimize their content accordingly.

Increased Website Traffic: Improved search engine rankings can increase website traffic.

More Leads and Sales: Increased website traffic can lead to more leads and sales.

Reduced Marketing Costs: Surfer SEO can help businesses reduce their marketing costs by helping them optimize their content for search engines.

Scalability: Surfer SEO is scalable and can be used by businesses of all sizes.

4. Revealbot

What is Revealbot?

Revealbot is a powerful AI-driven ad optimization tool designed to automate your ad management tasks, supercharging your campaigns and freeing you to focus on achieving results faster.

How Does Revealbot Work?

Revealbot offers a suite of features that cater to the needs of advertisers and agencies:

Automated Ad Management: It automates routine operations, allowing you to optimize your campaigns efficiently.

Campaign Scaling: With Revealbot, scaling your ad campaigns becomes hassle-free. Increase your ad spend with confidence, knowing Revealbot continually optimizes your efforts.

Custom Metrics: Tailor your analytics to match your unique business goals.

Pre-built Automation: Explore a range of pre-built automation strategies designed to enhance your ad campaigns. These strategies are ready to deploy and can be customized to suit your needs.

Revealbot's Benefits:

Revealbot's efficiency lies in its automated processes and intelligent insights:

Setup and Integration: Integrate your advertising accounts, such as Facebook Ads, with Revealbot—the tool syncs with your campaigns and ad sets.

Automation: Leverage Revealbot's extensive library of pre-built automation strategies or create custom rules. These rules define how Revealbot manages your ad campaigns.

Real-time Optimization: Revealbot continuously monitors your ad campaigns in real-time. It identifies underperforming ads and automatically reallocates your budget to high-performing ones.

Creative Insights: Optimize your ads for better engagement and conversions.

Improved Reach: Refine your targeting to reach the most receptive audience.

Reporting: Keep everyone in the loop with regular updates on your campaign's progress.

Easy Ad Creation: Perform creative and audience testing to fine-tune your campaigns for maximum impact.

5. AdCreative.ai

What is AdCreative.ai?

AdCreative.ai is a cutting-edge AI-driven platform that revolutionizes how businesses and marketers create ad content. It's a secret weapon for generating highly effective ads that boost conversions and save precious time.

How Does AdCreative.ai Work?

AdCreative.ai is a game-changer for brands, agencies, and businesses seeking to enhance their digital advertising efforts:

AI-generated Ad Creatives: AdCreative.ai specializes in crafting ads that sell, delivering results that exceed traditional methods.

Increased Conversions: AdCreative.ai's data-driven approach can lead to up to 14 times higher conversion rates than non-data-backed creatives.

Time Efficiency: Let AI handle the heavy lifting, freeing you to scale your campaigns and focus on strategic decisions.

Seamless Branding: AdCreative.ai understands your brand's colors and fonts, creating designs that seamlessly fit your branding.

Platform Integration: AdCreative.ai seamlessly integrates with major platforms like Google, Facebook, ADYOUNEED, and Zapier, making it adaptable to your advertising ecosystem.

AdCreative.ai's Benefits:

AdCreative.ai's innovation lies in its data-driven AI processes:

Creative Collection: AdCreative.ai compiles a vast database of high-conversion-rate ad creatives from prominent social and display platforms.

Creative Analysis: Each gathered creative is analyzed, generating over 80 data points per image. This analysis informs the AI about what works.

Machine Learning: AdCreative.ai's unique machine learning model learns from the data points and creative performance, refining its ability to predict high-converting ad content.

Creative Generation: The generative AI swiftly generates ad creatives, ranking them based on their anticipated conversion rates. This process ensures the most effective ads rise to the top.

Key Features

Super Scalable: Whether you need one creative or thousands, AdCreative.ai is built to accommodate your ad creative needs.

Text Generator: Get results-focused text and headlines tailored to your advertising platform, letting AI be your copywriter.

Creative Insights: See which creatives perform best across your ad accounts and gain inspiration for future campaigns.

Whitelabel Ready: Customize AdCreative.ai with your branding to make it uniquely yours.

Complete Ad Package: Let AI understand your product or service, create a strategy, and deliver ad creatives, texts, and audiences—all in one project.

Video Ads: Generate conversion-focused video ads for high ROI with the only AI capable of creating ready-touse videos.

Who Can Use It?:

AdCreative.ai is versatile and caters to various business types:

Startups: Spend your ad budget on creatives that convert, leveraging the strongest AI in ad creation.

E-commerce: Generate custom creatives and banners for your entire product catalog with the help of machine learning.

Agencies: Produce ad creatives and banners that deliver up to 14 times better conversion rates for your entire client portfolio.

Enterprises: Keep your ad creatives on-brand, gain AI insights into visuals, and streamline collaboration between your team and agency.

Action Steps: Crafting a Successful AI-backed Marketing Campaign

1. Set Clear Objectives
2. Data Integration with Adverity
3. Create a Data-Driven Strategy
4. Keyword and Hashtag Analysis with Brand 24
5. Analyze Competitor Data
6. AI-Generated Ad Creatives with AdCreative.ai
7. Monitor and Measure
8. Optimize in Real-Time

> *Now, I want to share my insights and expertise on utilizing artificial intelligence (AI) to enhance your marketing campaigns. I'll guide you through setting precise goals, selecting the right AI tools and strategies, and even providing real-world examples of businesses leveraging AI to achieve their marketing objectives.*

1. Setting Clear Objectives Using SEMrush

The first step in any successful digital marketing campaign is clearly defining your goals. What do you want to achieve with your campaign?

Do you want to:

Increase brand awareness?

Boost sales?

Generate leads?

Improve customer engagement?

Drive traffic to your website?

Improve your search engine ranking?

Once you know your goals, you can start to develop a marketing strategy that will help you achieve them.

Use AI Tools to Identify Your Goals

Many AI tools can help you identify your digital marketing goals. One such tool is SEMrush. SEMrush offers a variety of features that can help you analyze your competitors and identify keywords relevant to your target audience.

Please note that SEMrush is a comprehensive tool with many features, so I'll give you an overview of the critical steps involved.

1. Account Creation

Go to the SEMrush website and click the "Sign Up" button.

Choose your preferred subscription plan (SEMrush offers a free trial with limited features).

Provide the required information to create your account, including your email address and password.

Complete the registration process and log in to your SEMrush account.

2. Dashboard Overview

After logging in, you'll be directed to the SEMrush dashboard. This is your control center for all SEMrush features.

Familiarize yourself with the navigation menu on the left-hand side, which includes options like "Domain Analytics", "Keyword Research", "Backlink Analysis", and more.

3. Competitor Analysis

To set clear objectives, start by analyzing your competitors. Click on "Domain Analytics" and then "Overview".

Enter the domain of your main competitor and click "Search".

SEMrush will provide a wealth of data about your competitor's online presence, including their top organic keywords, paid search advertising, and backlinks.

4. Keyword Research

To understand the keywords relevant to your industry, click "Keyword Research" in the navigation menu.

Enter a seed keyword or phrase related to your business.

SEMrush will generate a list of related keywords, along with data on search volume, competition, and more.

5. Backlink Analysis

Assess your competitor's backlink strategy by clicking "Backlink Analytics" in the navigation menu.

Enter your competitor's domain to see where their backlinks are coming from.

Analyze the quality of these backlinks and identify potential opportunities for your link-building strategy.

6. Goal Setting

Based on your competitor analysis, keyword research, and backlink analysis, you can now set clear objectives.

Your objectives may include increasing organic traffic, improving search engine rankings, or enhancing your backlink profile.

Use the data from SEMrush to create specific, measurable, achievable, relevant, and time-bound (SMART) goals.

Monitor your progress within SEMrush using the various reports and tools available to track your performance.

7 Ongoing Optimization

Continuously use SEMrush to monitor your progress and adjust your digital marketing strategy as needed.

Regularly check your rankings, traffic, and backlinks to ensure you're on track to meet your objectives.

Utilize SEMrush's reporting features to create custom reports that showcase your progress to stakeholders.

> *After using SEMrush, you are equipped to set your goal and ready to launch a successful marketing campaign. The key to a successful marketing campaign is merging and understanding the data to create a data-driven strategy. The following section will guide you through this process. Just keep following the step-by-step instructions. You're on the right track.*

2. Data Integration with Adverity

The next step is to use Adverity to integrate data from various sources, such as advertising platforms, CRM systems, and web analytics. Create a unified data repository for analysis.

The purpose of data integration with Adverity is to consolidate and harmonize data from various sources, enabling comprehensive analysis and data-driven decision-making in marketing.

1. Create an Adverity Account

Visit Adverity Website: Open your browser and go to the Adverity website.

Sign Up: On the Adverity homepage, locate the "Sign Up" or "Free Trial" button, typically found in the top right corner. Click on it to initiate the account creation process.

Provide Account Information: You will be prompted to provide basic information to create your Adverity account. This typically includes details such as your name, email address, and a secure password. Fill in these details accurately.

Agree to Terms: Carefully read Adverity's terms of service and privacy policy. Once you've reviewed and agreed to these terms, check the box indicating your acceptance.

Complete Sign-Up: After agreeing to the terms, click the "Sign Up" or "Create Account" button to finalize your account creation.

2. Access Your Adverity Account

Confirmation Email: Shortly after creating your account, you will receive a confirmation email from

Adverity at the email address you provided during registration.

Open Confirmation Email: Access your email inbox and open the confirmation email sent by Adverity.

Click on Confirmation Link: Inside the email, you will find a link to confirm your email address and activate your Adverity account. Click on this link.

Log In: After confirming your email, you'll be redirected to the Adverity website. Use the email address and password you provided during registration to log in to your newly created Adverity account.

3. Begin Data Integration

Once logged in, you'll land on the Adverity dashboard. This is the central hub where you'll manage your data integration and analytics.

a. Access Data Integration.

Locating the Data Integration Section: After logging into your Adverity account, you'll need to find the section or option that enables you to initiate data integration or set up data sources. This section is typically within the Adverity dashboard, where you manage your data-related activities.

Dashboard Navigation: Look for a tab, link, or button on the dashboard menu or toolbar related to data integration. Standard labels for this section may include "Data Integration", "Data Sources", "Data Connections", or something similar. It's often found in a prominent location for ease of access.

Initiating Data Integration: Once you've located the data integration section, click on it to initiate the data integration process. This action will open up a series of options and settings that allow you to configure how data from various sources will be brought into Adverity.

b. Choose Data Sources

Selecting Data Sources: After accessing the data integration section, you will be prompted to choose the specific data sources you want to integrate into Adverity. Data sources can include a wide range of platforms and systems, such as advertising platforms (e.g., Google Ads, Facebook Ads), customer relationship management (CRM) systems (e.g., Salesforce, HubSpot), web analytics tools (e.g., Google Analytics), and more.

Checkboxes or Dropdown Menus: Adverity typically presents data source options in checkboxes, dropdown menus, or a combination of both. You'll see a list of available data sources that you can select for integration.

Selecting Relevant Sources: Carefully review the list of data sources and click on the checkboxes or drop-down options next to those relevant to your analytics objectives. For example, if you want to analyze the performance of your digital advertising campaigns, you might select data sources like Google Ads, Facebook Ads, and Google Analytics.

Customizing Data Sources: Depending on your specific requirements, you may also have the option to customize data sources. This could involve providing login credentials, API keys, or configuring settings to establish a connection between Adverity and each chosen data source.

Confirming Selections: Once you've selected the data sources you wish to integrate, there is often a "Next" or "Continue" button to confirm your selections and proceed to the next steps of the data integration process.

Review and Edit: Before finalizing your data source selections, take a moment to review your choices to ensure they align with your analytics goals. You may also be able to edit or modify your selections if needed.

c. Connect Data Sources

Follow On-Screen Instructions: Once you've selected your data sources, Adverity will guide you through connecting each source. Follow the on-screen instructions and prompts to establish the connections. Here's a more detailed explanation of what this might involve:

Providing Login Credentials: For some data sources, you may need to enter login credentials (username and password) associated with that source. This is common for platforms like Google Ads, Facebook Ads, or CRM systems.

API Key Integration: Data integration often requires an API (Application Programming Interface) key. If a data source uses an API for data access, you must generate an API key from that source and input it into Adverity. Adverity will provide fields or prompts where you can enter these keys.

Configuring Source Settings: Depending on the data source, you may need to configure specific settings to establish the connection. This could include specifying the data range, selecting the data type (e.g., advertising campaign data), and setting up data retrieval frequency (e.g., daily, weekly).

Authentication: Some sources may require additional authentication methods, such as OAuth tokens or client IDs. Adverity will guide you through the authentication process to ensure a secure connection.

Testing Connections: After entering the necessary information, Adverity often provides a testing mechanism to verify that the connection is successful. This ensures that data can be retrieved from the source without issues.

d. Data Mapping:

Understand Data Fields: Data mapping involves associating the data fields from each connected source with corresponding fields in Adverity's data repository. Before you start mapping, it's essential to have a clear understanding of the data fields available in each source. These fields can include metrics like clicks, impressions, and conversion rates and dimensions like campaign names, dates, and audience segments.

Access Data Mapping Tools: Adverity typically provides intuitive tools and interfaces for data mapping. These tools enable you to visually map data fields from your connected sources to their corresponding fields within Adverity's data structure.

Select Source and Destination Fields: For each data field in your connected sources, you'll select a corresponding field in Adverity where the data should be imported. This process involves linking the source field to the appropriate destination field. For instance, you'd map "Clicks" from Google Ads to the "Clicks" field in Adverity.

Transformations and Data Cleanup: Data mapping tools in Adverity often allow for data transformations and cleanup. This can include data type conversions, calculations, and filtering to ensure the data aligns correctly with your analytics objectives.

Validation and Testing: Before finalizing the data mapping, it's good practice to validate your mappings by testing the data import. Adverity may offer a preview option to check how the data will be integrated. This step helps identify and rectify any mapping issues.

Save Mapping Configurations: Once you're satisfied with the mapping, save the configuration. Adverity typically saves mapping templates, making it easier to apply the same mapping logic to future data imports from the same source.

Scheduled Updates: Additionally, Adverity often offers scheduling options for data updates. You can set a frequency for data retrieval (e.g., daily or weekly) to keep your data repository up-to-date.

e. Data Transformation

Depending on your requirements, you can apply data transformation and cleansing rules to ensure data consistency and accuracy.

f. Schedule Data Updates

Set regular data update schedules to keep your repository up-to-date with fresh information from your integrated sources.

g. Save Configuration

Once you've completed data integration and mapping, save your configuration settings.

2. Data Analysis

a. Access Data Repository

Navigate to Data Repository: Upon successful data integration and mapping, you can easily access your unified data repository within Adverity. This is where all the data from various sources is combined and made available for analysis.

User-Friendly Interface: Adverity typically provides a user-friendly interface for accessing the data repository. You'll find a dedicated section or dashboard where your integrated data is organized and ready for exploration.

b. Analyze Data:

Select Data for Analysis: In the data repository, you can select the specific datasets or data sources you want to analyze. Adverity allows you to choose the most relevant data for your analytical objectives. This selection flexibility is beneficial when you're working with extensive datasets.

Utilize Data Analysis Tools: Adverity offers a wide range of data analysis tools and features to support your analytical needs. Here's how you can utilize these tools:

a. **Data Visualization:** Create visual representations of your data, including charts, graphs, and dashboards. Adverity often offers drag-and-drop tools for building customized visualizations. This helps you identify trends, patterns, and anomalies quickly.

b. **Custom Metrics and Calculations:** Customize your analysis by defining specific metrics and calculations. Adverity allows you to create custom formulas and metrics tailored to your campaign or business objectives.

c. **Filtering and Segmentation:** Refine your analysis by applying filters and segmenting the data. This is especially useful for comparing the performance of different campaigns, time periods, or audience segments.

d. **Cross-Channel Analysis:** Adverity excels in crosschannel analysis. You can compare data from various advertising platforms, CRM systems, and web analytics to gain comprehensive insights into your marketing efforts.

e. **AI-Driven Insights:** Some versions of Adverity may incorporate AI-driven insights. These insights can automatically identify significant trends, anomalies, and opportunities within your data.

f. **Generate Reports:** Adverity generates comprehensive reports based on your analysis. You can typically customize these reports to include the specific metrics, visualizations, and insights you want to share with your team or stakeholders.

Benefits of Data Analysis with Adverity:

Data-Driven Decision Making: Having Adverity is a superpower that lets you make smart choices for your business. Empowers datadriven decision-making. You can make informed choices based on real-time and past data, leading to brilliant marketing campaigns and strategies.

Performance Optimization: By analyzing data across channels and sources, it shows you exactly where your campaigns are shining and where they need a little polish. This optimization leads to increased ROI and efficiency.

Visibility and Transparency: Adverity's data analysis tools provide transparency into your marketing performance. You can easily keep an eye on important merits, monitor campaign progress, and share insights with team members or clients.

Time Savings: Like a trusty assistant Adverity streamlines the data analysis process, saving you valuable time. You can perform complex analyses quickly and efficiently, allowing you to focus on strategy and decision-making rather than on mundane tasks like manual data manipulation.

Scalability: As your marketing efforts grow, Adverity scales with you, allowing you to grow without limits. You can add new data sources, create custom analytics, and adapt your reporting as your business expands.

Cross-Channel Insights: Adverity's magic lies in gathering data from all corners of the universe (okay, maybe just the internet). It can integrate data from multiple sources and give you cross-channel insights that are often challenging to achieve with individual analytics tools. This 360-degree view of your marketing efforts is invaluable for strategic planning.

3. Create a Data-Driven Strategy

Creating a data-driven strategy means leveraging insights from data analysis to make informed decisions and optimize marketing efforts for better results.

1. Navigate to Insights:

Look for a section or option on the dashboard that provides insights or data analysis tools. This might be labeled as "Insights" or "Analytics".

2. Select Data Sources:

Choose the data sources you want to analyze for insights. This can include advertising platforms, CRM systems, web analytics, and more.

3. Generate Insights:

Use Adverity's AI-powered analysis tools to generate insights from the selected data sources. This can include identifying trends, customer behavior patterns, and areas for campaign improvement.

4. Review AI Recommendations:

Adverity may provide AI-generated recommendations based on the data analysis. Pay attention to these recommendations, as they can inform your strategy.

5. Identify Key Trends:

Analyze the data to identify key trends in customer behavior, campaign performance, and other relevant metrics.

6. Develop a Strategy:

Based on the insights gathered, formulate a data-driven marketing strategy. This strategy should outline specific actions based on the identified trends and opportunities.

7. Set Objectives and KPIs:

Define clear objectives for your data-driven strategy.

Ensure that these objectives are specific, measurable, and aligned with the insights from Adverity.

8. Plan Campaign Adjustments:

Determine how you will adjust your marketing campaigns to align with the data-driven strategy. This might include changes to ad targeting, messaging, or budget allocation.

9. Implement and Monitor:

Put your data-driven strategy into action and closely monitor the results. Adverity may offer tools for tracking the performance of your campaigns in real-time.

10. Iterate and Optimize:

Continuously review the data and AI insights from Adverity. Use this information to improve your marketing strategy for ongoing success.

11. Measure and Report:

Regularly measure key performance indicators (KPIs) to gauge the effectiveness of your data-driven strategy. Adverity might provide reporting features to help you visualize and communicate your results.

4. Keyword and Hashtag Analysis with Brand24

Now, let's talk about our little eavesdropper. The purpose of keyword and hashtag analysis with Brand24 is to monitor and analyze online conversations, track brand mentions, and gain reports on customer sentiment, enabling data-driven decision-making for marketing campaigns.

1. Create a Brand24 Account:

Visit the Brand24 website.

Locate the "Sign Up" or "Try for Free" option on the homepage and click on it.

Fill in the required details to create your account. This typically includes your name, email address, and password.

Brand24 will send a verification email to the address you provided. Check your email inbox and click the verification link to confirm your email address.

Return to the Brand24 website and use your newly created credentials to log in to your Brand24 account.

2. Set up Keyword and Hashtag Monitoring:

Once logged in, you will be directed to your Brand24 dashboard.

Look for an option to create a new project or monitoring campaign. This is where you'll set up keyword and hashtag tracking.

Give your project a name that reflects its purpose, such as the name of your campaign or the keywords you want to monitor.

In the project setup, you can define the specific keywords and hashtags you want to monitor. Enter the keywords and hashtags that are relevant to your campaign.

Select the sources from which you want Brand24 to collect data. This can include social media platforms, blogs, news websites, forums, and more.

Configure alert settings to receive notifications in realtime when your defined keywords and hashtags are mentioned online. This allows you to stay updated on relevant conversations.

3. Monitor and Analyze Data:

After setting up your project, access the project dashboard within Brand24.

Brand24 will continuously monitor the web for mentions of your specified keywords and hashtags in real-time. You can view these mentions on your dashboard.

Click on individual mentions to analyze them further. Evaluate sentiment (positive, negative, neutral) and gather insights into customer opinions and competitor mentions.

Use Brand24's tools to track trends related to your campaign keywords and hashtags. Identify popular topics and discussions.

If needed, you can export data and insights from Brand24 for more in-depth analysis or reporting purposes.

4. Take Action:

Engage with users who mention your brand or campaignrelated keywords and hashtags. Respond to customer inquiries and address concerns promptly.

Based on the insights gathered from Brand24, consider adjusting your campaign strategy. This could involve refining messaging, targeting, or content.

Continuously measure the impact of your campaign and keyword monitoring efforts. Assess changes in sentiment, brand visibility, and engagement.

5. Analyze Competitor Data

Analyzing competitor data using Brand24 is a way to gain insights into competitors' online presence, customer sentiment, and trends. Allowing you to identify opportunities to differentiate your marketing campaign and gain a competitive edge.

1. Login to Your Brand24 Account:

Open your web browser and go to the Brand24 website.

Click on the "Login" button.

Enter your login credentials (username and password).

Click "Login" to access your Brand24 dashboard.

In your Brand24 dashboard, you'll see a list of projects you've set up. Select the project related to the competitor analysis you want to conduct.

2. Configure Competitor Monitoring:

Within your selected project, navigate to the "Sources" or "Competitors" section, configuring competitor monitoring.

Click on "Add Competitors" or a similar option.

3. Enter Competitor Information:

In the pop-up window, enter the names or URLs of the competitors you want to monitor.

You may also have the option to specify additional details about each competitor, such as their industry or location.

4. Adjust Monitoring Settings:

Customize the monitoring settings as needed. You can set up alerts for specific mentions related to your competitors, select the social media platforms to monitor, and choose the frequency of updates.

5. Save Competitor Settings:

After configuring the settings, click "Save" or a similar button to add your competitors to the monitoring list.

6. View Competitor Mentions:

Once the competitor monitoring is set up, Brand24 will start collecting and displaying mentions of your competitors from various online sources.

You can access these mentions in the "Mentions" or "Results" section of your project dashboard.

7. Analyze Competitor Data:

Review the mentions of your competitors to gain insights into their online presence, customer sentiment, and any trends or discussions related to them.

Pay attention to the sentiment analysis, which categorizes mentions as positive, negative, or neutral.

Look for patterns and opportunities to inform your marketing strategy and help you differentiate your campaign.

8. Export Data (Optional):

Brand24 typically provides options to export data or reports for further analysis or sharing with your team.

If needed, use the export feature to save relevant competitor data for reference.

9. Act on Insights:

Based on the insights from competitor data analysis, make informed decisions to adjust your marketing campaign.

Identify areas where you can differentiate your campaign and stand out in the market.

6. AI-Generated Ad Creatives with AdCreative. ai

When you're in charge of creating ads for your business, you want them to be eye-catching and powerful, but you also need them to work like a charm. That's where AdCreative.ai comes to the rescue! It's like having a creative genius by your side. You feed it information, and it magically crafts ads that grab attention and boost your campaign's success. AdCreative.ai uses artificial intelligence to produce highly effective and tailored advertisements that optimize campaign performance, save time, and improve ROI.

1. Sign Up and login on AdCreative.ai:

If you haven't already, visit the AdCreative.ai website.

Click on the "Sign Up" or "Create Account" button.

Provide the required information to create your account, including your name, email address, and password.

Verify your email address.

Use your newly created credentials to log in to your AdCreative.ai account.

2. Access AI-Generated Creatives:

Once logged in, you'll be directed to the dashboard.

Look for an option or button that creates AI-generated creatives. This may be labeled as "Create Ad Creatives", "Generate Ads", or something similar.

3. Choose Ad Type:

Select the type of ad you want to create. AdCreative.ai may offer options for various ad formats, such as social media posts, display ads, or video ads.

4. Input Insights from Brand24:

Refer to the insights gathered from the keyword and hashtag analysis using Brand24.

Incorporate relevant keywords, phrases, and insights from competitor analysis to inform your ad creative.

5. Customize Ad Elements:

Use AdCreative.ai's interface to customize ad elements such as text, headlines, images, and ad copy.

You can also specify the platform where you intend to run the ad (e.g., Facebook, Instagram, Google Ads, etc.).

6. AI-Powered Creativity:

Let the AI algorithms of AdCreative.ai work their magic. The platform will use data-driven insights and creative analysis to generate ad creatives tailored to your campaign objectives.

AI-Powered Creativity in AdCreative.ai represents the heart of this innovative tool. Here's a deeper dive into this process:

Data-Driven Insights: AdCreative.ai utilizes advanced AI algorithms to process your input data, including keywords, competitor insights, and campaign objectives. These algorithms have been trained on vast datasets to understand what ad elements drive engagement and conversions.

Understanding Audience Behavior: The AI algorithms analyze data patterns, including consumer behavior, preferences, and trends. By tapping into past and real-time data, they can identify what types of ad creatives are most likely to resonate with your target audience.

Contextual Analysis: The AI considers the context of your campaign, including the platform where the ad will run, the audience demographics, and the competition. It tailors the ad creatives to fit the specific context, ensuring they align with the platform's best practices.

Creative Analysis: AdCreative.ai's AI goes beyond essential keyword matching. It understands the nuances of language and creative elements. It can identify which ad headlines, visuals, and copywriting styles will most likely capture attention and drive action. Hence, it brings more traction to your business.

Personalization: One of the strengths of AI-powered creativity is personalization. The algorithms can create multiple ad variations to suit different audience segments. This means you can reach diverse groups within your target audience with messages that resonate specifically with them.

Speed and Efficiency: Unlike human designers and copywriters, AI operates at incredible speed. It can generate multiple ad creatives in minutes, saving you valuable time and effort. Who doesn't want their digital storefronts to be busy and with the least hard work?

Creative Freedom: While the AI handles the heavy lifting of generating ad creatives, it still allows human input and customization. You can review and edit the generated creatives to align them with your brand voice and specific campaign goals.

7. Review and Edit:

Sift through the AI-generated ad creatives. Ensure they align with your branding, messaging, and campaign goals.

Edit or make adjustments if needed.

8. Generate Ad Creatives:

Click the "Generate" or "Create" button to have AdCreative.ai generate the AI-backed ad creatives based on your inputs and insights.

9. Download or Export:

AdCreative.ai will provide the generated ad creatives in various formats suitable for your chosen advertising platforms.

Download or export the creatives to your computer or your advertising accounts.

10. Launch Ad Campaign:

Use the AI-generated ad creatives in your advertising campaigns on the respective platforms.

Set your targeting parameters, budget, and schedule per your campaign strategy.

11. 7. Monitor and Measure

Various AI tools can be used to monitor and measure the performance of your ads in real-time. However, I suggest Adverity because it provides a comprehensive analytics platform that integrates data from various sources and offers advanced analytics capabilities. It empowers marketers to monitor and measure campaign performance in real-time, make data-driven decisions, and optimize strategies for better results.

1. Access Adverity Dashboard:

Log in to your Adverity account.

2. Navigate to Analytics:

Look for a section or option on the dashboard that is related to analytics or performance tracking. It may be labeled as "Analytics", "Performance", or something similar.

3. Select Campaign:

Choose the specific campaign you want to monitor and measure. This could be a campaign related to a particular product, service, or marketing initiative.

4. Configure Analytics:

Adverity provides a range of analytics tools and features. Configure your analytics settings to align with the key performance indicators

(KPIs) you want to track. This could include click-through rates (CTR), conversion rates, return on investment (ROI), and more.

5. Set up Data Integration:

If you haven't already integrated the necessary data sources (e.g., advertising platforms, web analytics), ensure they are integrated into Adverity. This will provide real-time data for analysis.

6. Real-Time Monitoring:

Use Adverity's real-time monitoring capabilities to track your campaign's performance as it happens. You can view metrics and data in real-time to assess how your campaign is performing.

7. Data Analysis:

Dive into the analytics tools provided by Adverity. Analyze the data to gain insights into your campaign's performance. Look for patterns, trends, and areas where improvements can be made.

8. Adjust Your Strategy:

Based on the insights you gather from the analytics, make data-driven decisions. If you identify underperforming aspects of your campaign, consider making adjustments. This could involve refining ad creatives, changing targeting parameters, or reallocating the budget.

9. Create Reports:

Adverity generates reports summarizing your campaign's performance. Create a dashboard to highlight the KPIs that are most important to your team or stakeholders.

10. Continuous Monitoring:

Campaign performance can change over time, so it's crucial to assess whether your strategy meets your goals and adapt as needed.

8. Optimize in Real-Time

1. Access Adverity Insights:

Log in to your Adverity account and navigate to the insights or analytics section.

2. Review Performance Metrics:

Utilize Adverity's analytics capabilities to review the performance metrics of your campaign. Pay attention to critical indicators like click-through rates (CTR), conversion rates, and return on investment (ROI).

3. Analyze Brand Mentions and Sentiment:

Refer to the insights gained from Brand24 regarding brand mentions, competitor mentions, and customer sentiment. Identify emerging trends, positive or negative sentiments, or opportunities to engage with your audience.

4. Evaluate AdCreative.ai Recommendations:

If you've created ad creatives using AdCreative.ai, review any recommendations provided by the platform based on its AI analysis. This could include suggestions for ad copy, imagery, or targeting adjustments.

5. Identify Optimization Opportunities:

Based on the insights gathered from Adverity, Brand24, and AdCreative.ai, identify optimization opportunities. Look for areas where your campaign can be improved, such as targeting adjustments, creative refinements, or budget reallocations.

6. Adjust Budgets:

In your advertising platforms (e.g., Google Ads, Facebook Ads), access the budget settings for your campaign. Consider reallocating budgets to channels or campaigns performing well or increasing budgets for highperforming ads.

7. Refine Targeting:

Review your targeting parameters, such as audience demographics and interests. Make adjustments based on the insights you've gained to reach your ideal audience segments better.

8. Optimize Ad Creatives:

If AdCreative.ai has provided recommendations, apply these optimizations to your ad creatives. This could involve modifying ad copy, imagery, or headlines to align with the data-driven insights.

9. Implement Real-Time Changes:

Use the advertising platforms' dashboards to implement the changes you've identified. This may involve pausing underperforming ads, launching new creatives, or adjusting bidding strategies.

10. Monitor Real-Time Impact:

After making the real-time optimizations, closely monitor the impact on your campaign. Monitor performance metrics to see how the changes affect CTR, conversion rates, and other KPIs.

11. Iterate and Test:

Optimization is an ongoing process. Continue to iterate and test different strategies based on the insights you gather. A/B testing can be particularly valuable for finetuning your campaigns.

12. Document and Report:

Document the optimizations you've made and their impact on the campaign's performance. Create reports summarizing the changes and improvements achieved through real-time optimization.

Hypothetical Example: Nina's Niche Marketing Marvel Using AI Tools

Nina, an ambitious entrepreneur, set out to expand her unique jewelry line to new markets in different countries. However, expanding internationally presented unique challenges, including understanding diverse market trends, monitoring brand reputation, and crafting compelling ad campaigns. Recognizing the potential of AI-powered marketing tools, she leveraged Adverity, Brand24, and AdCreative.ai to achieve remarkable success in her international expansion. The challenges she planned to tackle with the use of AI were:

Market Diversity: Entering new markets meant facing diverse consumer preferences and trends.

Brand Reputation: Nina needed to maintain a positive online reputation and address customer sentiments promptly.

Creative Marketing: Crafting ad creatives that resonated with each target market while maintaining brand identity was crucial.

Nina saw the value of AI-powered marketing and used it to her advantage. Nina created an Adverity account and integrated data from various sources, including social media, e-commerce platforms, and web analytics, to gain insights into market trends and customer behavior in each target country.

Using Brand24, Nina monitored keywords and hashtags related to her niche jewelry business across multiple countries. This allowed her to track brand mentions, competitor mentions, and customer sentiment in real-time.

Nina utilized Brand24 to gain insights into her competitors' online presence and customer sentiment. This helped her identify opportunities to differentiate her campaign and offerings.

Armed with insights from Brand24 and Adverity, Nina used AdCreative.ai to generate AI-backed ad creatives tailored to each target market. The platform's data-driven recommendations ensured her campaigns were compelling and effective.

Nina engaged with her audience by responding to mentions promptly using the insights from Brand24. She addressed both positive comments to strengthen her brand and negative comments to protect her online reputation.

Nina's strategic use of AI-powered marketing tools yielded outstanding results:

Global Expansion: Nina successfully expanded her jewelry business to multiple countries, catering to diverse customer preferences.

Brand Reputation: With real-time social listening through Brand24, Nina managed to protect her brand's reputation by addressing concerns promptly.

Increased Conversions: AI-generated ad creatives from AdCreative.ai led to increased click-through rates and conversions in each target market.

Competitive Edge: By analyzing competitor data with Brand24, Nina identified opportunities to differentiate her products and marketing strategies.

Nina's journey from a local artisanal jewelry business to an international success story showcases the transformative power of

AIdriven marketing tools. Adverity, Brand24, and AdCreative.ai played pivotal roles in her niche marketing marvel, allowing her to navigate market diversity, protect her brand reputation, and craft creative campaigns that resonated with global audiences. Her success serves as a testament to the potential of AI tools for expanding businesses across borders.

Checklist for the Modern AI-Backed Digital Marketer

Set Clear Objectives

Define Campaign Goals:

- ☐ Specify the Primary Objectives
- ☐ Identify Target Markets
- ☐ Establish KPIs

Data Integration with Adverity:

- ☐ Create an Adverity Account
- ☐ Select Data Sources
- ☐ Connect Data Sources

Create a Data-Driven Strategy

- ☐ Analyze Integrated Data
- ☐ Leverage AI Insights
- ☐ Develop a Comprehensive Strategy

Keyword and Hashtag Analysis with Brand24:

- ☐ Access Brand24 Dashboard
- ☐ Monitor Keywords and Hashtags
- ☐ Generate Reports

☐ Identify Trends and Areas for Improvement in Your Campaign

Analyze Competitor Data:

☐ Competitor Tracking

☐ Analyze Competitor Mentions

☐ Identify Opportunities

☐ Adjust Your Strategy Based on Competitor Strengths and Weaknesses

AI-Generated Ad Creatives with AdCreative.ai:

☐ Access AdCreative.ai

☐ Generate AI-Backed Ad Creatives

☐ Incorporate Brand Insights

Monitor and Measure:

☐ Access Analytics Dashboard

☐ Continuously Monitor

Optimize in Real-Time

☐ Gather Real-Time Insights

☐ Adjust Campaign Elements

☐ Optimize for Maximum Impact

"*Opportunities don't happen. You create them.*"

- Chris Grosser

CHAPTER 4

AFFILIATE MARKETING: LET AI CHOOSE FOR YOU

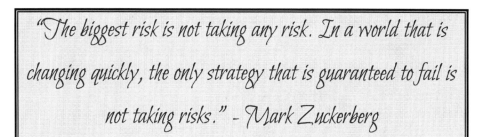

"The biggest risk is not taking any risk. In a world that is changing quickly, the only strategy that is guaranteed to fail is not taking risks." - Mark Zuckerberg

The Premise of Affiliate Marketing

Want to make money online without spending a dime? If so, affiliate marketing could be the perfect solution for you. Affiliate marketing is a performance-based marketing strategy where you earn commissions by promoting the products or services of other businesses. This means that you can earn money even if you don't have your own products or services to sell. Affiliates earn commissions for each sale, click, or action generated through their marketing efforts. It's like being a digital matchmaker, connecting eager customers with valuable products.

Let's explore affiliate marketing and its incredible potential.

The Affiliate Marketer's Role

Picture this: You have a blog, a vibrant YouTube channel, or a thriving social media presence. You've cultivated an engaged audience interested in your niche. Now, you can leverage your influence by becoming an affiliate marketer.

Your role is to introduce your audience to products or services relevant to their interests. You'll do this by creating content—blog posts, videos, reviews, or social media posts—that showcases these offerings. You'll include unique tracking links provided by the affiliate program to ensure you receive credit for any conversions.

Affiliate Marketing Potential: The Sky's the Limit

So, what makes affiliate marketing so appealing? Here's a glimpse into its boundless potential:

Accessible to All: Affiliate marketing doesn't discriminate. Whether you're a seasoned marketer or a passionate hobbyist, you can join the affiliate ranks. It's a level playing field for all.

Flexible Income: Your earnings aren't capped by a fixed salary. Your income potential is as flexible as your dedication and creativity. Successful affiliates often enjoy multiple streams of income.

Passive Earning: You can create a high-quality blog post or video review that continues to attract visitors and generate sales months, even years, after its creation.

That's the power of passive income in affiliate marketing.

Low Risk, High Reward: Unlike starting a brick-and-mortar business, affiliate marketing requires minimal upfront investment. You won't handle inventory, customer support, or shipping logistics. Your focus is on promotion.

Global Reach: The internet transcends geographical boundaries. Your affiliate efforts can reach a global audience, amplifying your earning potential exponentially.

Diverse Niches: Whether you're passionate about tech gadgets, wellness products, finance, or travel, there's an affiliate program tailored to your niche. You can promote products you genuinely believe in.

Continuous Learning: Affiliate marketing is an everevolving field. It's an opportunity to continuously learn and adapt to new strategies, technologies, and market trends.

Community and Support: Thriving affiliate networks and communities offer support, mentorship, and a wealth of resources to help you succeed.

Affiliate marketing is more than a revenue stream; it's a journey of self-discovery and innovation. It's about understanding your audience's needs, building trust, and making informed recommendations. It's the art of creating valuable content that enriches lives and, in turn, enriches yours.

Here's a step-by-step breakdown of the premise of affiliate marketing:

1. Parties Involved: There are three key parties involved in affiliate marketing:

Merchants or Advertisers: These businesses have products or services to sell.

Affiliates or Publishers: Individuals or entities promote the merchant's products on their platforms.

Customers: These consumers make purchases through the affiliate's promotional efforts.

2. Affiliate Promotion

Affiliates promote the merchant's products through various marketing channels, such as blogs, websites, social media, email marketing, or even paid advertising.

3. Unique Tracking Links

To track affiliates' performance, unique tracking links are generated for each affiliate. These links ensure the merchant can identify which sales or leads originated from a specific affiliate's efforts.

4. Commission Structure

Merchants decide on a commission structure, which can be a percentage of the sale price, a fixed amount per sale, or a combination of both. This commission is paid to affiliates only when a desired action is completed, such as a sale, lead, or click-through.

5. Performance Metrics:

Both merchants and affiliates closely monitor key performance metrics like clicks, conversions, conversion rates, and earnings per click (EPC) to evaluate the effectiveness of the affiliate marketing campaign.

6. Payment to Affiliates:

Affiliates receive their earnings as commissions based on the agreed upon terms. Payments can be made regularly, such as monthly or bi-weekly.

How AI Can Pinpoint Profitable Products and Trends

Artificial Intelligence (AI) is crucial in optimizing affiliate marketing campaigns by helping affiliates identify profitable products and trends. Here's how AI achieves this:

1. Data Analysis:

AI systems can analyze vast amounts of data, including historical sales data, customer behavior, and market trends. By processing this data, AI can identify which products or niches are currently trending and can potentially be profitable.

2. Predictive Analytics:

AI algorithms can predict future trends and consumer preferences based on historical data. This enables affiliates to focus their efforts on promoting products or services with a higher likelihood of generating sales.

3. Keyword Research:

AI-powered tools can perform in-depth keyword research to uncover relevant keywords and search trends. Affiliates can use this information to create content that aligns with what consumers are actively searching for.

4. Competitor Analysis:

AI can help affiliates analyze their competitors' strategies, including the products they promote and the keywords they target. This competitive intelligence can guide affiliates in making informed decisions.

5. Personalization:

AI can personalize marketing campaigns based on individual customer preferences and behavior. This increases the chances of converting visitors into customers by offering those products they are more likely to be interested in.

6. Performance Optimization:

AI can continuously optimize marketing campaigns by adjusting ad placements, content, and targeting based on real-time data, ensuring maximum profitability.

Brandon's List of Prerequisites for Affiliate Marketing

Before diving into the tools, I want you to know the prerequisites for affiliate marketing so they don't get lost in the technicalities.

Moreover, don't get overwhelmed by these. In the next section, I have provided straightforward step-by-step instructions on how to do it:

1. **Website or Blog:** You need a platform to promote affiliate products. This could be a website, blog, or social media profile.

2. **Domain and Hosting:** If you opt for a website or blog, you'll need a domain name (your website's address) and hosting (a server to store your website files).

3. **Affiliate Programs:** Sign up for affiliate programs that align with your niche. Research and choose programs that offer products or services your audience is interested in.

4. **SEO Knowledge:** Basic knowledge of Search Engine Optimization (SEO) helps your content rank higher in search engine results, driving organic traffic to your site.

5. **Social Media Presence:** Utilize social media platforms to promote your content and engage with your audience.

6. **Analytical Tools:** Set up tools like Google Analytics to track your website's performance and understand user behavior.

7. **Content Strategy:** Develop a content plan that includes the types of content you'll create, posting frequency, and promotion strategies.

8. **Patience and Persistence:** Affiliate marketing takes time to generate significant income. Be patient and persistent in your efforts.

9. **Budget:** While it's possible to start with minimal investment, having a budget for tools, advertising, and website maintenance can be beneficial.

10. **Monetization Strategy:** Plan how you'll monetize your website through affiliate marketing, whether it's through product reviews, banner ads, or other methods.
11. **Adaptability:** Be prepared to adapt to changes in the affiliate marketing landscape, including shifts in consumer behavior and platform policies.

Tools Spotlight: AI-driven Affiliate Dashboards and Analytics

Affiliate marketing is a great way to make money online. But it can be overwhelming to know where to start. That's why I'm here to introduce you to some of the best tools and resources for affiliates. These tools will help you with everything from managing partnerships to optimizing ad campaigns and analyzing data. So, whether you're a beginner or a seasoned pro, I encourage you to check them out. Let's briefly touch upon a few of them:

Niche Research Tools: Uncovering a profitable niche is the first step in affiliate marketing success. Tools like Google Trends, SEMrush, or Ahrefs can provide insights

into trending topics and keyword opportunities.

Content Creation and SEO Tools: Crafting compelling content is at the heart of affiliate marketing. Tools like Grammarly, Yoast SEO, or BuzzSumo can help you polish your content and improve its search engine visibility.

Now let's look at the affiliate marketing platforms where opportunity awaits you.

1. Skimlinks

Skimlinks is a powerful platform designed to empower publishers by transforming their content into a sustainable source of revenue through commerce content. In a world that's becoming less reliant on traditional ads, commerce content offers a way for editorial teams to monetize their valuable content effectively.

What is Skimlinks For?

Skimlinks serves the crucial purpose of enabling publishers to monetize their content through affiliate marketing seamlessly. Here's how it accomplishes this:

Access to a Vast Network of Affiliate Programs:

Skimlinks provides access to an impressive network of affiliate programs, totaling 48,500 programs, all conveniently accessible in one place. These programs come from 50 different networks, including CJ, Awin, and Rakuten Advertising.

What sets Skimlinks apart is its ability to negotiate exclusive rates with merchants. These negotiated rates often surpass the usual rates by a significant margin. In fact, a remarkable 41% of publishers' revenue comes from these exclusive rates that Skimlinks secures.

Comprehensive Analytics Suite:

Skimlinks offers a robust Publisher Hub, which includes a wide range of insightful reports. Publishers can access reports such as performance by merchant, real-time clicks, and revenue sources.

By analyzing the performance of different types of content with their audience, media publishers can optimize their strategies to generate more revenue. For added flexibility, Skimlinks provides a reporting API that allows you to import commerce data into your business intelligence tools.

Automated Affiliate Links:

One of the key features of Skimlinks is its ability to automate the monetization of commerce links. After implementing a piece of code on your website and AMP pages, Skimlinks works its magic by automatically converting your regular commerce links into affiliate links.

This means that you can start earning commissions from over 48,500 merchants effortlessly. It frees up your time to focus on what you do best—creating exceptional content.

Testimonials:

Skimlinks has garnered praise from reputable publishers, including the Daily Mail, Radio Times, and Dotdash. Users appreciate its user-friendly Editor Toolbar, which makes it easy to identify merchants offering increased rates.

Forms of Commerce Content:

Skimlinks supports various forms of commerce content, ranging from evergreen product reviews to gift guides and timely deals. This versatility enables publishers to experiment and diversify their content offerings.

Tools for Editorial Teams:

Skimlinks equips editorial teams with essential tools such as the Editor Toolbar, Link Wrapper, and AMP integration. The AMP integration is especially valuable, ensuring that mobile users don't miss out on revenue opportunities.

In summary, Skimlinks is a game-changer for publishers looking to monetize their content effectively in a world where traditional advertising is evolving. It provides access to a vast network of affiliate programs, negotiates exclusive rates, offers comprehensive analytics, and automates turning regular commerce links into profitable affiliate links.

2. Impact

Impact.com is a global partnership management platform that has recently launched a new tool called impact.com/creator. This tool serves as an all-in-one influencer marketing platform designed to help advertisers discover, create, manage, and scale influencer programs within one interface. It aims to bridge the gap between influencer and affiliate marketing, providing a simplified way for brands to enter the influencer space.

What Is Impact.com for:

Impact.com offers a wide range of solutions for publishers:

1. Create - Find Publishing Partners:

Impact.com enables publishers to discover thousands of revenue-generating partnerships. You can easily find publishing partners that align with your audience and content.

Connect with brands directly through the Impact.com marketplace. This direct partnership approach monetizes your content effectively. Discover top brands that resonate with your audience's preferences and optimize these partnerships with Impact.com's publisher automation suite.

2. Grow - Generate Revenue with Commerce Content:

The platform empowers publishers to generate revenue through commerce content. It uses data to give you useful information about your audience, how well your content is doing, your efforts, and your commerce endeavors.

Impact.com provides a centralized location for analyzing your audience, content, and commerce performance across numerous networks. This transparency allows you to make informed decisions and watch your revenue grow.

3. Diversify - Diversify Your Partner Portfolio:

Partnerships with brands come in various forms, and Impact.com recognizes this diversity. Sponsored content raises awareness, commerce content drives purchasing decisions, and loyalty and cashback programs help seal the deal.

Impact.com for Publishers assists you in highlighting the unique value you bring to brand partnerships, extending your influence beyond the last click.

4. Monetize - Monetize Your Content:

Impact.com simplifies the process of monetizing your existing content. With its innovative tools and continuous partnership solutions, you can effortlessly earn additional revenue from your content.

By putting content monetization on autopilot, Impact. com ensures you can focus on scaling your business and carving your distinctive path in a world of competition

5. How Impact.com Works:

Impact.com centralizes your social, website, and affiliate data from over 200 channels and networks into one convenient place. This eliminates the need to log in and out of multiple platforms, saving you precious time.

The platform's tools gather and organize your data, allowing you to focus on what truly matters—creating engaging content.

Impact.com provides insights into your audience's behavior, helping you understand where they spend the most time, which articles are most popular, and which parts of your site generate the most profit.

It offers tools to create new affiliate links in seconds and fix broken ones quickly, helping you recapture lost revenue.

Impact.com also provides live reports that enable you to impress your brand partners with comprehensive data on the performance of your content and partnerships.

3. Awin

Awin is a global affiliate marketing network that enables individuals and businesses to establish profitable partnerships with some of the world's leading brands. It provides a platform where affiliates can promote products and services to their respective audiences, ultimately earning commissions for driving sales and conversions.

What is Awin for:

Awin's network boasts several impressive statistics:

£1.1 billion earned by affiliates last year: Awin affiliates collectively earned over £1.1 billion in commissions, highlighting the platform's potential for revenue generation.

260 affiliates join their network daily: A growing community of affiliates continually joins Awin, showcasing its attractiveness and effectiveness as an affiliate marketing platform.

25,000 brands on their network across all sectors: Awin collaborates with various brands from various industries, ensuring affiliates can find partners that align with their target audience.

Who can benefit from the Awin Platform?

The Awin platform benefits a diverse range of individuals and businesses involved in affiliate marketing and online promotion. Here are the primary beneficiaries of the Awin platform:

Affiliates: Affiliates are individuals or entities that promote products and services from advertisers to their audience. They earn commissions for driving traffic, leads, or sales to the advertiser's website. Awin provides affiliates with a vast network of brands to partner with, trackable links, and a platform for managing their affiliate marketing efforts.

Content Creators: Bloggers, vloggers, social media influencers, and website owners who create content and have an audience can benefit from Awin. They can monetize their content by partnering with relevant advertisers and earning commissions on referred sales.

Digital Marketing Agencies: Digital marketing agencies that manage online advertising and promotional campaigns for clients can use Awin to access a wide array of affiliate programs. This diversifies their services and can boost client revenue via affiliate partnerships.

E-commerce Businesses: E-commerce businesses can leverage Awin to set up their own affiliate programs, enabling them to reach a broader audience and boost sales. This is particularly valuable for businesses looking to expand their online presence.

Publishers: Online publishers, including news websites, lifestyle magazines, and niche blogs, can incorporate affiliate marketing as an additional revenue stream. They can partner with Awin's advertisers and earn commissions by promoting relevant products or services within their content.

Advertisers and Brands: Advertisers and brands looking to expand their online reach can collaborate with Awin to tap into a network of affiliates and publishers. Awin offers tools and resources to help brands create and manage successful affiliate programs.

Individual Entrepreneurs: Individuals interested in starting an online business or side hustle can explore affiliate marketing through Awin. They can select advertisers whose products align with their interests or expertise and earn commissions on sales.

Marketing Professionals: Marketing professionals seeking to broaden their skill set and generate additional income can use Awin to delve into the affiliate marketing world. Awin's user-friendly platform makes it accessible to marketing experts and beginners alike.

Key Benefits of Awin:

Faster and More Consistent Payments: Awin ensures that affiliates receive payments for validated transactions, regardless of when Awin receives compensation from the advertiser. This minimizes payment delays and provides financial stability to affiliates.

Intuitive, Easy-to-Use Platform: Awin's user-

friendly platform simplifies the management of affiliate campaigns. It offers clear labels, consistent layouts, effective tools, and a comprehensive reporting suite. Whether you're an individual blogger, influencer, or part of a digital marketing team, Awin's platform is designed to support your marketing operations.

Expert Support Team: Awin provides dedicated support through its Publisher Development and Partner Success teams. These teams offer regional commercial expertise and assistance with optimizing advertiser partnerships. The Partner Success Center is a valuable resource for answering publisher questions and supporting Awin's tools and solutions.

How Affiliate Marketing Works with Awin:

Connect with the Right Advertiser Brands:

Affiliates can explore the Advertiser Directory on Awin

to discover brands that align with their audience. This directory can be filtered by sector, making it easier to find suitable partners.

Promote Your Audience: Affiliates can effortlessly generate trackable links or images through the Awin interface. These promotional assets can be added to websites, blogs, or social media accounts to promote individual products, services, or advertiser brands.

The Visitor Follows the Link: Affiliates encourage and influence their website visitors to click through to the advertiser's site using the provided links. All visits from the affiliate's site are tracked and recorded within the Awin dashboard.

Get Commission from Sales: When visitors referred by affiliates make approved purchases on the advertiser's site, the affiliate earns commissions. The Awin platform records these transactions, providing detailed information on order value and earned commissions.

Action steps: Setting Up and Scaling an Affiliate Business with AI

1. Niche Research with SEMrush
2. Select Affiliate Programs with Skimlinks
3. Content Creation with Jasper
4. SEO Optimization with SurferSEO
5. Performance Tracking and Optimization

1. Sign Up for SEMrush Account

1. Set Up Account

Open your web browser and go to the Semrush website. Click the "Get started" or "Sign up for free" button to create a new account.

Fill in the required information, including your name, email address, and password.

Complete the registration process by following the onscreen prompts.

Once you've registered and logged in, you'll be taken to the SEMrush dashboard.

2. Start Niche Research

In the SEMrush dashboard, you'll find a search bar at the top. Enter a broad topic or industry you're interested in exploring for your niche. For example, if you're interested in pet care, you can start with "pet care".

3. Analyze Organic Search Results

SEMrush will provide you with an overview of the organic search results for your chosen topic. Look for keywords with high search volume and reasonable competition.

Click on the "View full report" or similar option to access a detailed list of related keywords.

4. Keyword Analysis

In the keyword report, you can see a list of keywords related to your chosen niche. Monitor metrics like search volume, keyword difficulty, and CPC (Cost Per Click).

Sort the keywords by search volume to identify highdemand keywords within your niche.

Use filters to narrow down your search. For example, you can filter by keyword difficulty to find manageable competition.

5. Competitor Analysis

Explore the "Competitors" or "Competitive Analysis" section in SEMrush to identify the top websites and competitors in your niche.

Analyze competitor websites to understand their content strategies, top-performing keywords, and backlink profiles. This will help you gain insights into what works in your niche.

6. Trend Analysis

Navigate to the "Trends" or "Market Trends" section in SEMrush to discover trends related to your niche.

Explore historical and current trends to understand the seasonality and popularity of topics within your chosen niche.

7. Select Your Niche

Based on your research, choose a niche within your broader topic that aligns with your interests and has profitable keywords with manageable competition.

Make a note of the high-demand keywords and trends you've identified to guide your content creation.

2. Select Affiliate Programs with Skimlinks

1. Sign Up for Skimlinks

Open your web browser and go to the Skimlinks website.

Click the "Join Now" or "Sign Up" button to create a new Skimlinks account.

2. Complete the Registration Process

Fill in the required information, including your name, email address, and password.

Agree to the terms and conditions and click the "Sign Up" or "Join Skimlinks" button.

Follow any additional on-screen prompts to verify your email address and complete your registration.

3. Access Your Skimlinks Dashboard

Once you've registered and logged in, you'll be taken to your Skimlinks dashboard.

4. Explore Affiliate Programs

In your Skimlinks dashboard, navigate to the section or tab that lists available affiliate programs. This may be labeled as "Affiliate Programs", "Merchants", or something similar.

Skimlinks provides access to a vast network of affiliate programs across various industries.

5. Search for Affiliate Programs

Use the search bar or filters provided by Skimlinks to find affiliate programs that align with your niche or your audience's interests. You can search by keywords, categories, or industries.

Browse through the list of available programs and read their descriptions to determine if they offer products or services that your audience will value.

6. Review Program Details

Click on the affiliate program's name or description to access more details.

Review important information such as commission rates, cookie durations, and any specific terms or requirements the program sets.

Consider the program's relevance to your niche and the potential earnings it can generate.

7. Join Affiliate Programs

If you find an affiliate program that suits your niche and audience, click on the "Join Program" or "Apply" button associated with that program.

Follow the application process, including providing additional information or agreeing to specific program terms.

8. Await Approval

Once you've applied to an affiliate program, you may need to wait for the program administrator to review and approve your application.

Check your email regularly for notifications regarding your application status.

9. Access Affiliate Program Tools

After approval, you'll typically gain access to affiliate program tools, including affiliate links, banners, and marketing materials.

Use these tools to promote the products or services of the affiliate program to your audience.

3. Content Creation with Jasper

1. Access the Jasper Platform

Open your web browser and go to the Jasper website (or log in if you already have an account).

2. Sign In or Create an Account

If you're not already signed in, click the "Sign In" or "Log In" button.

If you don't have an account, click the "Sign Up" or "Create an Account" option to register.

3. Explore Content Ideas

Once logged in, navigate to the section or tool that allows you to explore content ideas. This may be labeled as "Content Ideas", "Topic Generator", or something similar.

Enter relevant keywords or topics related to your niche searched in step 1 using SEMrush.

4. Review Content Suggestions

Jasper will generate a list of content topic suggestions based on your keywords.

Browse through the suggestions to identify topics that resonate with your target audience or address their needs and questions.

5. Select a Content Idea

Choose a content idea that you'd like to explore further. Consider factors like relevance, search demand, and competition.

6. Create Your Content

Click on the selected content idea to access more details and insights.

Use this data to craft a well-structured article, review, or guide. Ensure your content is informative, engaging, and valuable to your audience.

Write a compelling headline and introduction to capture readers' attention.

7. Add Visuals and Media

Enhance your content with images, videos, infographics, or other multimedia elements.

Ensure that visuals are relevant to the topic and provide additional value to readers.

8. Proofread and Edit

Carefully proofread your content to eliminate grammatical errors and typos.

Edit for clarity, coherence, and readability.

9. Publish or Save as Draft

Depending on your content management system (CMS), you can either publish your content immediately or save it as a draft for further review.

10. Promote Your Content

Share your newly created content on your website or blog.

Promote it on social media, email newsletters, and other relevant channels to reach your target audience.

4. SEO Optimization with SurferSEO

1. Access the SurferSEO Platform

Open your web browser and go to the SurferSEO website.

If you already have an account, sign in. If not, you may need to create a new account and subscribe to a suitable plan.

2. Start a New SEO Audit

Once you're logged in, navigate to the SEO Audit tool. This tool is typically located in the main dashboard or menu.

3. Enter Your Website URL

In the SEO Audit tool, enter the URL of the web page or content you want to optimize. SurferSEO will analyze this page for SEO improvements.

4. Initiate the Audit

Click the "Start Audit" or similar button to begin the analysis process.

5. Review the SEO Audit Report

SurferSEO will generate a comprehensive SEO audit report for the specified webpage.

Pay attention to key elements such as keyword usage, content structure, meta tags, and other on-page SEO factors.

The audit report will recommend optimizing these elements based on data-driven insights.

6. Keyword Analysis

Analyze the keyword recommendations provided by SurferSEO. These recommendations may include suggestions for additional keywords to include in your content.

Evaluate keyword density and ensure it aligns with best practices.

7. Content Structure Optimization

Follow SurferSEO's recommendations regarding content structure. This may involve adjusting headings, subheadings, and paragraph lengths to enhance readability and SEO performance.

Ensure that your content flows logically and coherently.

8. Meta Tags Optimization

Review and optimize meta tags, including the title tag and meta description, based on SurferSEO's suggestions.

Craft compelling and keyword-rich meta tags to improve click-through rates in search results.

9. Content-Length and Quality

Assess SurferSEO's recommendations for content length and quality. Make the necessary adjustments to meet the suggested criteria.

Ensure that your content provides valuable information to your audience.

10. Audit Score

Take note of the overall audit score that SurferSEO has provided. This score reflects the SEO health of your content.

11. Implement Changes

Based on the audit report, implement the recommended changes to your content. This may involve editing the existing content, adding new sections, or adjusting meta tags.

Save your changes.

12. Re-audit and Monitor

After implementing the recommended optimizations, initiate a re-audit using SurferSEO.

Compare the new audit report with the previous one to gauge the improvements in on-page SEO.

13. Track Progress

Continue to monitor the performance of your optimized content using SurferSEO's tracking features.

Keep an eye on your search engine rankings, organic traffic, and other relevant metrics.

5. Performance Tracking and Optimization

1. Sign Up for Google Analytics

Open your web browser and go to the Google Analytics website (analytics.google.com).

Sign in with your Google account or create a new one if you don't have one.

Click the "Start measuring" button to begin setting up Google Analytics.

2. Create a New Property

In the Admin section, click "Create Property" under the Property column.

3. Configure Property Settings

Choose between a "Web" or "App" property depending on your needs (for website tracking, select "Web").

Enter the Property name (e.g., Your Website Name).

Enter the Website URL.

Select your Industry Category and Reporting Time Zone.

Click the "Create" button to create the property.

4. Get the Tracking Code

After creating the property, you'll receive a tracking code snippet. This code needs to be added to your website's HTML.

5. Install the Tracking Code on Your Website

Copy the tracking code snippet provided by Google Analytics.

Paste the code snippet into the HTML of every page on your website just before the closing </head> tag.

Save your website's HTML files and ensure the code is implemented correctly.

6. Verify Tracking

Return to Google Analytics and click "Next" on the setup page.

Google Analytics will start tracking your website's data. It may take some time before data is visible in your reports.

7. Accessing Performance Data

Once data starts coming in, you can access it by clicking on "Reports" in the left-hand menu of your Google Analytics dashboard.

Explore various reports to monitor your website's performance, including audience demographics, acquisition sources, user behavior, and more.

8. Set up Google Search Console Integration

Go to Google Search Console.

Sign in with the same Google account used for Google Analytics.

Click on your website property (you should see it listed).

In the Search Console, click "Settings" in the left menu, then "Google Analytics property".

Click "Add" and select your Google Analytics property.

Click "Save".

9. Access Data in Google Search Console

In Google Search Console, you can access data related to your website's performance in Google search results.

View search queries, click-through rates, impressions, and more to gain insights into your website's appearance in Google searches.

10. Analyze and Optimize

Regularly review the data from Google Analytics and Google Search Console to analyze user behavior, traffic sources, keyword performance, and more.

Use these insights to make data-driven decisions to optimize your website's content, user experience, and SEO strategy.

Hypothetical Example: Omar's Affiliate Achievements Using AI

Omar, a dedicated affiliate marketer with a passion for beauty products. He had a knack for knowing which concealers would work best for different skin types and tones, and he was always up-to-date on the latest trends. Omar ventured into affiliate marketing to promote ladies' concealer products. Armed with a well-thought-out strategy and a suite of powerful tools, Omar achieved remarkable success in this competitive niche. This case study highlights how he leveraged specific AI tools and techniques to become a top-performing affiliate marketer in the beauty industry.

Omar's interest in beauty products and cosmetics led him to explore affiliate marketing in the beauty niche. He recognized that the ladies' concealer market presented an opportunity due to its evergreen demand and the potential for high commissions.

Omar began his journey by conducting thorough niche research using SEMrush. He identified valuable keywords related to concealer products, gauged search demand, and assessed competition. This research allowed him to pinpoint profitable keywords and trends within the beauty niche.

To monetize his content effectively, Omar signed up for Skimlinks. He leveraged this platform to access affiliate programs, including top beauty brands offering concealer products. Skimlinks made it convenient for him to find and join relevant affiliate programs seamlessly.

Omar understood that content was crucial for building trust with his audience. He utilized Jasper, a content creation tool, to craft highquality articles, reviews, and guides on various concealer products. His informative and engaging content positioned him as a trusted authority in the beauty niche.

To ensure his content reached a wider audience, Omar optimized it for search engines using SurferSEO. This data-driven tool provided insights on keyword usage, content structure, and meta tags, which helped improve his rankings in search engine results.

He employed Google Analytics to monitor his website's performance. This tool provided valuable data on user behavior, traffic sources, and conversions. It allowed him to assess the effectiveness of his affiliate marketing efforts and make data-driven decisions.

Omar focused on creating content aligned with high-performing keywords he identified through SEMrush. This content included in-depth product reviews, tutorials, and comparisons of different concealer brands. By catering to user search intent, he attracted organic traffic to his website.

Within his well-researched content, he strategically placed affiliate links using Skimlinks. These links directed users to the respective product pages of the concealer brands. His transparent and honest reviews encouraged click-throughs and conversions.

SurferSEO played a pivotal role in optimizing Omar's content. He meticulously fine-tuned on-page SEO elements, ensuring his articles ranked higher in search engine results pages (SERPs). This led to increased visibility and organic traffic.

With Google Analytics, Omar continuously monitored the performance of his affiliate marketing campaigns. He tracked key metrics such as traffic, conversion rates, and revenue generated from affiliate sales. This data allowed him to identify top-performing content and optimize underperforming ones.

Omar's dedication to affiliate marketing in the ladies' concealer niche yielded impressive results:

His website became a go-to resource for beauty enthusiasts seeking concealer product recommendations and reviews.

Omar consistently ranked in search engine results, driving substantial organic traffic to his site.

Conversion rates for affiliate products were above industry standards, leading to a significant increase in commissions earned.

He expanded his affiliate partnerships with top beauty brands, negotiating exclusive commission rates through Skimlinks.

Monthly revenue from affiliate marketing surpassed his initial expectations, making it a lucrative source of income.

Omar's success in the beauty niche extended beyond affiliate marketing. Brands started reaching out to collaborate on sponsored content, further diversifying his revenue streams.

Omar's quest in affiliate marketing for ladies' concealer products is an inspiring example of how strategic planning, niche research, and the right tools can lead to outstanding achievements. By leveraging tools like SEMrush, Skimlinks, Jasper, SurferSEO, and Google Analytics, he not only established himself as a top affiliate marketer and makeup mogul but also built a sustainable and profitable empire in the competitive beauty industry. His commitment to delivering value through informative content and data-driven optimization strategies allowed him to flourish in a niche he is truly passionate about.

Checklist for the AI-Enhanced Affiliate Marketer

🖋AI-Generated Ad Creatives with AdCreative.ai:

- ☐ Access AdCreative.ai
- ☐ Generate AI-Backed Ad Creatives

🖋Niche Research with SEMrush:

- ☐ Sign Up for a SEMrush Account
- ☐ Identify Your Target Niche or Industry
- ☐ Analyze Keyword Search Volume and Competition
- ☐ Explore Competitor Websites and Their Top-Performing Keywords
- ☐ Compile a List of Profitable Keywords for Content Creation
- ☐ Select Affiliate Programs with Skimlinks.

🖋Create a Skimlinks Account

- ☐ Explore the Skimlinks marketplace
- ☐ Browse Affiliate Programs Related to Your Niche
- ☐ Join Affiliate Programs that Align with Your Niche and Audience
- ☐ Use Skimlinks to Generate Affiliate Tracking Links
- ☐ Place Affiliate Links Strategically Within Your Content

Content Creation with Jasper:

- ☐ Access the Jasper platform
- ☐ Use Jasper's Content Generation Tools to Create Articles, Reviews, or Guides
- ☐ Incorporate Relevant Keywords from Your SEMrush Research
- ☐ Proofread and Edit Your Content for Quality

SEO Optimization with SurferSEO:

- ☐ Sign up for a SurferSEO Subscription
- ☐ Conduct a Content Audit Using SurferSEO's Audit Feature
- ☐ Analyze Keyword Usage and Density
- ☐ Optimize On-page Elements Such as Meta Tags, Headings, and Images
- ☐ Implement SurferSEO's Recommendations for Content improvements
- ☐ Monitor Your Content's SEO Score and Make Adjustments as Needed

Performance Tracking and Optimization:

- ☐ Set up Google Analytics for Your Website
- ☐ Connect Google Analytics to Your Website Using a Tracking Code

☐ Monitor Website Traffic, User Behavior, and Conversion Rates in Google Analytics

☐ Use Google Analytics Data to Identify Top-performing Content and Affiliate Products

☐ Optimize Underperforming Content by Analyzing User Behavior

"Success usually comes to those who are too busy to be looking for it." - Henry David Thoreau

CHAPTER 5

BECOMING A WEBSITE DESIGNER WITH AI ASSISTANCE

"It's not about ideas. It's about making ideas happen."

- Scott Belsky

rtificial intelligence (AI) transforms how we live and work, and website design is no exception. AI can be used to streamline the design process, boost creativity, and enhance the overall user experience of websites.

In this chapter, we're diving into the art of becoming a website designer with a powerful ally by your side – artificial intelligence (AI).

Let's discover practical tools, techniques, and strategies to empower you to become a proficient website designer in this AI-driven era.

The Importance of Web Presence in Today's World

In today's digital age, having a strong web presence is no longer an option; artificial intelligence (AI) is transforming how we live and work, and website design is no exception. AI can be used to streamline the design process, boost creativity, and enhance the overall user experience of websites.

The world of website design is changing rapidly. In the past, website design was a manual process, requiring designers to understand HTML, CSS, and JavaScript deeply. But today, artificial intelligence (AI) is revolutionizing website design. AI has played a significant role in this evolution, revolutionizing the way designers work and the experiences they create.

Whether you're an individual, a business, or an organization, your website serves as your virtual storefront, and it often forms the first impression potential visitors, customers, or clients have of you. Here's why a robust web presence is crucial:

1. **Global Reach:** The internet knows no borders. A welldesigned website can reach a global audience, breaking down geographical limitations.

2. **Credibility and Trust:** A professional website enhances your credibility and builds trust with your audience. It signifies that you're a legitimate entity, whether it's for personal branding or business.

3. **24/7 Accessibility:** Unlike physical stores or offices, your website is accessible 24/7, allowing people to engage with your content, products, or services anytime.

4. **Marketing Hub:** Your website is a central hub for your digital marketing efforts. It's where you direct traffic from social media, email campaigns, and other online channels.

5. **Competitive Edge:** In a competitive market, having a welldesigned website can set you apart from competitors who may still lag in their online presence.

6. **Data Insights:** Websites provide valuable data and insights about user behavior, allowing you to refine your strategies and improve user experiences.

7. **Scalability:** Whether you're a small startup or a large corporation, your website can scale with your needs, accommodating growth and changes in your business.

AI's Role in Website Design: Speed, Aesthetics, and Functionality

Artificial intelligence is transforming the way websites are designed and maintained. It brings a plethora of benefits, enhancing various aspects of web development:

1. **Speed and Efficiency:** AI-powered tools streamline the design process, significantly reducing the time required to create and update websites.
2. **Aesthetics:** AI can analyze design trends and user preferences, helping designers create visually appealing websites that resonate with their target audience.
3. **Personalization:** AI enables dynamic content and personalization, tailoring the user experience to individual visitors based on their behavior and preferences.
4. **User Experience:** AI-driven chatbots and virtual assistants enhance user experiences by providing real-time assistance and support.
5. **Search Engine Optimization (SEO):** AI algorithms can analyze and optimize website content for search engines, improving visibility and ranking.

6. **Security:** AI helps identify and mitigate security threats, protecting websites from cyberattacks and data breaches.

7. **Analytics:** AI-driven analytics provide deeper insights into user behavior, helping businesses make data-driven decisions for website improvements.

8. **Content Creation:** AI can generate content, such as product descriptions or news articles, reducing the manual workload for content creators.

Tools Spotlight: AI Website Builders and Design Assistants

Gone are the days when you needed to be a coding wizard to create a website. Thanks to artificial intelligence (AI), anyone can now build a professional-looking website without technical knowledge.

AI website builders are using machine learning to automate many tasks involved in website creation, such as designing, developing, and optimizing websites. This makes it possible for anyone to create a website quickly and easily, even if they don't have any prior experience.

Here are some of the top AI website builders making waves in the market:

1. Wix ADI

Wix ADI (Artificial Design Intelligence) is a ground-breaking feature that the well-known website builder Wix offers. It's designed to make website creation incredibly easy, even for those without design or technical skills. Here's a brief overview:

What is Wix ADI for?

Effortless Website Creation: Wix ADI is primarily for individuals and businesses looking to create a website quickly and effortlessly.

Personalized Design: It is ideal for those who want a website that reflects their style and needs without delving into intricate design decisions.

Time and Cost Efficiency: It's a time-saving solution that can significantly reduce the time required to design and launch a website.

How Does Wix ADI Work?

Answer Questions: To start, you'll be asked questions about your website's purpose, industry, and style preferences.

AI Magic: Wix ADI's AI algorithm uses your responses to analyze your needs and generate a website design tailored to you.

Customization: Once the initial design is ready, you have the flexibility to customize it further. You can add, edit, or remove elements as you see fit.

Content Integration: You can import your content, such as images and text, and Wix ADI will intelligently place them within the design.

Mobile Optimization: It ensures that your website is mobile-responsive, so it looks great on smartphones and tablets. In today's world, more and more people are using their smartphones and tablets to access the internet. If your website isn't mobile-responsive, you're missing out on many potential customers.

SEO Assistance: Wix ADI even provides SEO suggestions to help improve your site's visibility on search engines.

2. Zyro

Zyro is a user-friendly website builder that aims to simplify the website creation process for individuals and businesses. Here's a brief overview of what Zyro is for and how it works:

What is Zyro for?

Effortless Website Building: Zyro is designed for people who want to create a website quickly and easily with minimal technical expertise.

Small Businesses and Entrepreneurs: It's suitable for small businesses, startups, entrepreneurs, and individuals who need an online presence.

Budget-Friendly: Zyro is budget-friendly, making it a cost-effective choice for those who want a professionallooking website without breaking the bank.

How Does Zyro Work?

Choose a Template: Begin by selecting a template from Zyro's collection. These templates are designed for various industries and purposes.

Customize: Zyro's drag-and-drop editor customizes the chosen template. You can easily change colors, fonts, images, and text to match your brand or style.

Add Content: Populate your website with content. You can create and edit pages, add sections, and include essential elements like text, images, videos, and forms.

AI Tools: Zyro incorporates AI tools for various functions, such as AI content generator, logo maker, and more, to streamline the design and content creation process.

E-commerce Features: If you're setting up an online store, Zyro offers e-commerce features like product listings, shopping carts, and secure payment options.

Mobile Optimization: Zyro makes your website mobile-friendly, so it looks and functions perfectly on smartphones and tablets.

SEO Assistance: It provides SEO guidance and tools to help improve your website's visibility on search engines.

Publish: Once satisfied with your website, you can publish it with a click. Zyro also offers hosting services.

Zyro's simplicity and AI-powered features make it an accessible choice for those who want a professional website without the complexities of manual web design.

3. 10Web.io

10Web.io is an innovative AI-powered website builder designed to simplify and accelerate the website creation. Here's an overview of what 10Web.io is for and how it works:

What is 10Web.io for?

Efficient Website Building: 10Web.io is tailored for individuals and businesses looking to quickly create a professional website without the complexity of traditional web development.

AI-Generated Content: It's ideal for those who want AI-generated content and images to jumpstart their website, saving time and effort.

Customization: 10Web.io caters to users who want the flexibility to customize their website's design and content using an intuitive drag-and-drop editor.

E-commerce Growth: For e-commerce businesses, it offers features like product page customization, product description generation, inventory management, and order tracking.

How Does 10Web.io Work?

Website Generation with AI: To begin, users answer a few simple questions about their business. Based on these answers, AI technology generates tailored content and images for the website.

Customization: Users can customize the generated content and images to match their preferences and brand identity.

Page Addition: It allows users to add more pages to their website as needed, ensuring a complete online presence.

Drag-and-Drop Editing: 10Web.io offers a user-friendly drag-and-drop editor. Users can easily edit every website design element, ensuring it meets their exact specifications.

Premium Widgets: Users can access a range of premium widgets within the 10Web editor. These widgets cover various functions, layouts, marketing tools, and e-commerce features.

Website Publishing: Once the website is complete, users can publish it with ease.

Additional Features:

AI Website Builder Integration: The AI Website Builder integrates seamlessly into the website creation process, making it efficient and user-friendly.

E-commerce Solutions: For businesses, especially in the e-commerce sector, 10Web.io provides tools for product page customization, AI-generated product descriptions, and an easy-to-use dashboard for product management.

Scalability: Users can scale their e-commerce businesses with the help of 10Web's solutions, benefiting from reliability and performance. 10Web.io's integration of AI technology streamlines website creation, allowing users to create, design, and publish a custom website quickly and efficiently.

4. Durable.co

Durable.co is a cutting-edge AI website builder that enables users to create professional websites in a matter of seconds. Here's an overview of what Durable.co is for and how it works:

What is Durable.co for?

Rapid Website Creation: Durable.co is designed for individuals and businesses who need to establish a web presence quickly and easily.

AI-Powered Design: It offers AI-powered design capabilities suitable for various purposes, including graphic design, event planning, consulting, copywriting, recruiting, tutoring, and more.

Comprehensive Website Solution: Durable.co provides everything needed to get online, including hosting, analytics, and a custom domain name.

Professional Visuals: Users gain access to a vast library of professional photos and icons, allowing them to enhance the visual appeal of their websites effortlessly.

AI Website Editor: Durable.co's AI-powered website editor enables users to customize their sites with features like testimonials, scheduling, multiple pages, and built-in components. No coding skills are required.

SEO Optimization: The platform automatically generates SEO-friendly pages, optimizing websites for search engines to increase online visibility and attract more traffic.

Security: Durable.co strongly emphasizes security, ensuring that every website is protected with robust measures like DDOS protection, SSL, firewall, and a global CDN. This provides a worry-free experience.

How Does Durable.co Work?

Website Creation in Seconds: Users can create a website in a matter of seconds using Durable.co's AIdriven technology. The process is swift and efficient.

Customization: Durable.co's AI-powered website editor allows users to customize their sites to suit their needs and preferences. Whether it's adding testimonials, scheduling features, multiple pages, or built-in components, customization is a breeze.

Professional Visuals: Users can access a vast library of professional images and icons, automatically adding visual appeal to their websites.

SEO Optimization: Durable.co automatically generates SEO-friendly pages, ensuring that websites are easily discoverable by search engines.

Security: The platform prioritizes security, providing top-notch protection against DDoS attacks, SSL encryption, firewall security, and global content delivery network (CDN) support.

Durable.co simplifies the website creation process with its AIdriven approach, making it an ideal choice for individuals and businesses looking to establish an online presence quickly and without the need for extensive technical expertise.

5. Hocoos.com

HOCOOS is an innovative AI website builder designed to simplify creating a fully functional website for businesses. Here's a breakdown of what HOCOOS is for and how it works:

What is HOCOOS for?

Effortless Website Creation: HOCOOS is tailored for individuals and businesses seeking a hassle-free solution to build their online presence. It's perfect for startups, entrepreneurs, and anyone needing a website without the complexities of coding or design.

Customizable Content: The platform streamlines website development by generating custom content, including text, design, and images, based on your responses to eight quick questions.

Versatile Website Builder: HOCOOS isn't limited to just basic websites. It empowers users to create online stores, blogs, booking systems, and marketing platforms, providing a wide array of tools for business growth.

Real-Time Content Generation: Rather than assuming your needs, HOCOOS engages in a conversation with you about your business. As you provide information, it generates compelling written and visual content in real time, tailored to your specific requirements.

Human Support: While AI does the heavy lifting, HOCOOS ensures that real humans can provide support whenever you need assistance beyond what AI can offer.

How Does HOCOOS Work?

Simple Setup: Begin by answering eight straightforward questions about your business. This initial information serves as the foundation for your website.

AI Content Generation: It has an AI Content Creator that can generate high-quality written material for pages, blog posts, and articles. The content is tailored to your business and industry, and it is SEO-optimized to help you rank higher in search results. It can also create visual content, such as design elements and images.

Customization: You can customize and fine-tune the generated content to align with your brand and preferences.

Diverse Website Types: Whether you need an online store, a blog, a booking system, or a marketing platform,

HOCOOS accommodates your requirements.

Fast Website Deployment: HOCOOS accelerates getting your website online, saving you hours of tedious editing and design work.

Comprehensive Analytics: The platform offers features like total sales analytics and font selection, enhancing your website's functionality.

Future-Ready: HOCOOS empowers your business to embrace the future of online presence. It takes just five minutes to create a website that could have a transformative impact on your business.

HOCOOS combines the convenience of AI-generated content with the flexibility to tailor your website to your specifications.

Action Steps: Designing a Website from Scratch with AI

As a web developer with years of experience, I've tried a lot of different platforms for website creation. But Durable.co is my top pick for two reasons.

Firstly, it's incredibly easy to use. Even if you're a beginner, you can create a professional-looking website in minutes. Durable.co's AI-powered features do all the heavy lifting for you, generating content and designs tailored to your specific needs.

Secondly, it's perfect for e-commerce. Durable.co has a robust and user-friendly platform for selling products online. You can create a beautiful online store in no time, and Durable.co will take care of all the technical details.

Here's how Durable.co can help you create a professional website or online store:

1. Sign Up and Account Creation

Visit the Durable.co website

Look for the "Sign Up" or "Get Started" button on the homepage and click it.

You will be prompted to enter your email address and create a password. Fill in this information and click "Sign Up".

2. Answer Business-Related Questions

After signing up, you will be asked questions about your business or website idea. These questions help Durable. co understand your needs and preferences.

Provide detailed responses to these questions, which will be used to generate initial content for your website.

3. Customize Your Website

Once you've answered the initial questions, Durable.co's AI will generate a basic website.

Use the built-in website editor to customize your site further. You can change the layout, fonts, colors, buttons, and more.

Add specific components like customer reviews, image galleries, and contact forms as needed.

4. Choose Your Domain

Durable.co typically includes a custom domain with your subscription. You can choose a domain name that fits your business.

Follow the on-screen instructions to select and register your custom domain.

5. Add an Online Store (Optional)

If you plan to create an online store, look for the e-commerce features within Durable.co.

Follow the platform's guidelines to add and customize your online store. This may include adding product listings, prices, and descriptions.

6. Payment Integration (Online Store Only)

To accept payments on your online store, integrate payment gateways like PayPal, Stripe, or other supported options.

Configure your payment settings to ensure a smooth checkout process for customers.

7. SEO Optimization

Durable.co includes built-in SEO features to help optimize your website for search engines.

Pay attention to on-page SEO elements, such as keyword usage, meta tags, and content structure.

Use the platform's SEO optimization tools to improve your website's search engine rankings.

8. Review and Publish

Before publishing your website, thoroughly review all its elements, including content, design, and functionality.

Better safe than sorry.

Make any final adjustments or corrections as needed.

Once satisfied, click the "Publish" or "Go Live" button to make your website accessible to the public.

9. Monitor and Update

After your website is live, regularly monitor its performance using Durable.co's analytics tools.

Make updates and changes to your content or design to keep your website fresh and engaging.

Indeed, we're living in the era of AI-driven innovation, and the way we create websites has transformed significantly. Gone are the days when building a website was a complex and timeconsuming process that often required hiring agencies and months of development.

With the advancements in AI technology, everyone, regardless of their technical expertise, can now construct a website in a matter of hours. AI-powered website builders like the ones we'll explore in this book have made it possible to streamline the web development process, providing pre-designed templates, content generation, and even e-commerce integration at your fingertips.

It's an exciting time for aspiring web developers and entrepreneurs, as you can now bring your ideas to life online faster and more efficiently than ever before.

Hypothetical Example: Lisa's AI-Powered Web Design Journey

Lisa was just another aspiring web designer with big dreams. She loved creating beautiful and functional websites, but she simply didn't have enough hours in the day. As a new mother, her days were filled with caring for her baby, leaving her with very little time to pursue her dream of becoming a web designer.

But Lisa was determined, and she knew that in this era of AI, there had to be a way to make her dream a reality without sacrificing her time with her child. That's when she stumbled upon the power of AI website builders.

Lisa's journey began with a simple idea - creating a website for selling handmade baby accessories. She knew she had a unique product line, and she wanted a platform to showcase her creations to the world. However, her limited technical knowledge and time constraints were significant roadblocks.

After some research, Lisa chose Durable.co as her AI-powered website builder. It was the ideal choice for someone with minimal technical expertise, thanks to its intuitive interface and AI-driven features. With Durable.co, Lisa could create a professional-looking website without the need for coding or design skills.

Lisa started by signing up on Durable.co, and in a matter of minutes, she had her account up and running. The platform asked her questions about her business and design preferences. Lisa was amazed at how tailored the questions were to her specific needs.

The AI-powered builder generated a stunning design based on Lisa's preferences. She could easily customize it to match her brand's aesthetic. Colors, fonts, and layouts were all adjustable with a few clicks.

She uploaded product images, and Durable.io automatically optimized them for her website. She could add product descriptions effortlessly, thanks to AI-generated content suggestions.

With Durable.co, Lisa integrated an e-commerce store seamlessly into her website. It handled everything from product listings to secure payment processing, leaving her worry-free.

Durable.io didn't stop at design and functionality; it even helped Lisa with SEO. It generated SEO-friendly content and made her website visible to potential customers on search engines.

Her website looked like a top-tier agency had designed it, but the reality was that Lisa had created it herself with the help of AI.

In just a few days, Lisa's website was up. And her first order came in 22 days. Her baby accessories were available to a global audience. The response was overwhelming. Lisa's leap into the world of elite web design using AI not only allowed her to fulfill her dream but also opened up new revenue streams. She could balance her life as a mother and an entrepreneur, thanks to the power of AI-driven web design. In this era of AI, the only limit is your imagination, and Lisa proved that anyone can turn their dreams into reality with the right tools and determination.

Checklist for Future AI-Driven Web Designers

Define Your Goals and Niche

- ☐ Clearly Outline Your Website's Purpose and Objectives
- ☐ Identify Your Target Audience and Niche
- ☐ Analyze Keyword Search Volume and Competition

Research and Choose an AI-powered Website Builder

- ☐ Research AI website builders Like Durable.co, Wix ADI, Zyro, and 10web.io
- ☐ Select the Platform that Aligns with Your Goals and Design Preferences

Sign Up and Set Up Your Account

- ☐ Create an Account on Your Chosen AI Website Builder
- ☐ Follow the Platform's Setup Process, Including Domain Registration if Needed

Customize Your Design

- ☐ Use the AI's Design Features to Customize the Look and Feel of Your Website
- ☐ Choose Color Schemes, Fonts, and Layouts that Match Your Brand

Content Creation and Integration

- ☐ Add Content to Your Website, Including Text and Images
- ☐ Utilize AI-generated Content Suggestions to Enhance Your Copy
- ☐ If You're Running an e-commerce Site, Integrate Your
- ☐ Product Listings

SEO Optimization

- ☐ Optimize Your Website for Search Engines Using AIdriven SEO Tools
- ☐ Focus on On-page Elements Like Keywords, Meta Tags, and Content Structure

Test Responsiveness

- ☐ Ensure that Your Website is Responsive and Displays Correctly on Various Devices
- ☐ Test the Site's Load Times and Make Necessary Optimizations

E-commerce Integration (If Applicable)

- ☐ Set up Your Online Store, Including Product Listings and Payment Processing
- ☐ Ensure a Smooth and Secure Shopping Experience for Customers

✦ Launch and Promote

☐ Perform Final Testing to Ensure Everything is Functioning Correctly

☐ Announce the Launch of Your Website through Social Media and Email Marketing

✦ Monitor and Optimize

☐ Regularly Review Website Analytics to Identify Areas for Improvement

☐ Make Necessary Updates to Enhance User Experience and Achieve Your Goals

CONCLUSION

You have just witnessed how artificial intelligence (AI) is not just a trendy term; it is a real force that has the power to transform your online endeavors, increase your income sources, and move you closer to financial independence.

This extensive guide has shed light on the road to success in a wide variety of fields, from print on demand and self-publishing to digital marketing and affiliate promotion, all within the scope of a single book. Artificial intelligence's potential has been exposed, and it is at your disposal to start your online business today.

Now, as we conclude this extraordinary journey through the chapters of *Broke to Billionaire*, let's consider the path ahead. You've acquired valuable knowledge, insights, and tools that can shape your online ventures and transform your financial future. However, this is not the end; it's a new beginning.

Charting Your Path to Success

1. **Integration is Key:** Take the lessons from each chapter and see how they can complement each other. For example, use AI-driven content creation to enhance your social media presence or apply AI-enhanced video production to boost

your e-commerce store's product demonstrations. Integration amplifies your AI-powered strategies.

2. **Continuous Learning:** The field of AI is dynamic and ever-evolving. Stay updated with the latest AI technologies, tools, and trends. Attend webinars, workshops, and courses to expand your knowledge and stay at the forefront of AI innovation.

3. **Networking:** Connect with fellow AI enthusiasts, entrepreneurs, and professionals in your niche. Join online communities, attend conferences, and engage in meaningful conversations. Collaboration and knowledge sharing can open up new opportunities and insights.

4. **Data-driven decision-making:** Embrace data analytics as a crucial part of your AI-powered endeavors. Use AI tools to analyze user behavior, engagement metrics, and sales data. Data-driven insights will guide your strategies and lead to better outcomes.

5. **Ethical AI:** Always prioritize ethical AI practices. Ensure that your AI implementations align with legal and ethical standards. Be transparent with your audience about the use of AI in your processes.

6. **Mentorship:** Consider seeking mentorship from experts in your field. Learning from experienced individuals can fast-track your success and help you avoid common pitfalls.

7. **Scale and diversify:** As you see success in one area, consider scaling your efforts and diversifying your income

streams. Explore new platforms, markets, or niches where AI can be applied effectively.

8. **Patience and Persistence:** Remember that success may not happen overnight. It requires patience, persistence, and the willingness to adapt and learn from failures. Keep your long-term goals in sight and stay committed to your journey.

In conclusion, *Broke to Billionaire* is not just a book; it's a roadmap to a future where AI and human ambition harmonize to create unprecedented opportunities. Brandon Chan has not only equipped you with knowledge but has also ignited a spark within you. Now, it's your turn to take the reins, embrace the potential of AI, and chart your path to success in the ever-evolving digital landscape. The future is bright, and you have the tools to make it shine.

"The purpose of Life is a Life of Purpose"

- Robert Bryne

WATCH THIS SPACE AS BOOK 2 IS ON ITS WAY!!

It focuses on the following areas to further help with your journey to success:

» Social Media: Amplifying Outreach with AI
» Content Creation and Blogging are Boosted by AI
» E-commerce Store Optimization with AI
» Freelancing: AI as Your Ultimate Assistant
» Online Tutoring and Courses: Personalized with AI
» Video Production and Editing Enhanced by AI

Just as book 1, *Broke to Billionaire*, has been your trusted guide, the future books will further expand your horizons, providing indepth insights and practical guidance tailored to each domain. With Brandon Chan's expertise as your beacon, the world of AI is not just a promise; it's a journey filled with endless opportunities.

The future is yours to shape, and with AI as your ally, success knows no bounds.

"I find that the harder I work, the more luck
I seem to have." - Thomas Jefferson

THANK YOU

Dear Reader, Thank you for taking the opportunity to read my book. As much as I hope you enjoyed reading this book, I also hope it has given you the courage and confidence to embark on your new journey. I am so passionate about helping others understand the exciting future of AI that I would like to offer you a free copy of my *Billionaire Prompt book*. This book was written specifically to assist you in launching your new enterprise successfully. 100 prompts for each chapter of *Broke to Billionaire*. To get your free copy today, please click on this link, or better yet, use your phone's camera to scan this QR code.

https://preview.mailerlite.io/preview/43989/sites/104795318262 957838/mpoU5a

REFERENCES

How to use Midjourney to open an Etsy print-on-demand shop (no date): Growing Your Craft Available at: https://www.growingyourcraft.com/blog/how-to-use-midjourney-to-open-anetsy-print-on-demand-shop (Accessed: 17 September 2023).

Shaffer, C. (2023, March 15). How A.I. Art is an Etsy Print-On-Demand Game Changer: Brand Creators Brand Creators. https:// www.brandcreators.com/how-a-i-art-is-an-etsy-print-on-demandgame-changer/

Start publishing with KDP (n.d.). https://kdp.amazon.com/en_US/help/topic/GHKDSCW2KQ3K4UU4

Hopkins, E. (2023, September 1). A couple made $34,000 in 3 months selling books on Amazon KDP. Here's how they use ChatGPT to help write their books: Business Insider. https://www.businessinsider. com/how-to-sell-books-on-amazon-kdp-audible-ai-chatgpt-2023-9

Watch, M. (n.d.). 6 Benefits of using AI in Digital Marketing Metrics Watch. https://metricswatch.com/ai-in-digital-marketing

Phillips, A. (2023) 10 AI marketing tools your team should be using in 2023 Sprout Social. https://sproutsocial.com/insights/aimarketing-tools/

Vivek (2022, June 3). The Best AI Tools For Affiliate Marketing: How To Automate Your Processes. I Mean Marketing. https:// imeanmarketing.com/blog/ai-tools-for-affiliate-marketing/

Sawyer, B. (2023, April 24). How To Use AI For Affiliate Marketing | Travelpayouts. Travelpayouts Blog – Travel Partnership Platform. https://www.travelpayouts.com/blog/ai-affiliate-marketing/

Morris, C. (2023) 7 Best AI Website Builders in 2023 (for Fast Web Design) Elegant Themes Blog https://www.elegantthemes.com/ blog/marketing/best-ai-website-builders

Birch, N., & Valeanu, A. (2023). 16 Best AI tools for Web Designers.

Designmodo. https://designmodo.com/ai-tools-designers/

THE END

Made in the USA
Las Vegas, NV
11 December 2024

13868848R00127